THE REALLY PRACTICAL GUIDE TO PRIMARY ASSESSMENT

David and Wendy Clemson

Stanley Thornes (Publishers) Ltd

First published in 1991 by:
Stanley Thornes (Publishers) Ltd
Old Station Drive
Leckhampton
CHELTENHAM GL53 0DN
England

British Library Cataloguing in Publication Data
Clemson, David
The really practical guide to primary assessment.
1. Primary schools. Students, Academic achievement. Assessment
I. Title II. Clemson, Wendy
372.1264
ISBN 0–7487–0587–2

Typeset by Tech-Set, Gateshead, Tyne & Wear.
Printed and bound in Great Britain at The Bath Press, Avon.

Contents

Preface

The main assumption of this book is that whether you are doing assessments of the kind you have to do, or to inform your personal judgements, you will do them better with a range of information and skills at your fingertips. We have deliberately not tied all that we have written to the requirements of the law. Just as programmes of study and attainment targets are but a framework for teachers to accommodate, so too are the assessment arrangements. We are confident that teachers can be as creative in their assessing as they are in their teaching, and long after the introduction of the National Curriculum has been forgotten, teachers will still be continually fuelling their own judgements about children's performance and potential.

In the present educational climate, some teachers may be feeling a sense of loss: loss of status, public respect, parity with other professions and self confidence. People who experience loss are said to need not sympathy but support. This book attempts to give support by laying bare some of the important arguments in assessment, to fuel your thinking and discussion, and by giving you information to add to your professional knowledge and to enhance your confidence.

As we began writing each chapter, we found ourselves saying *this* is the heart of the book, *this* is the important chapter, *this* one will be *really* helpful to teachers. We trust that you agree with our convictions, and that you find that every chapter proves important in developing and refining your assessment expertise.

Dedication

This book is dedicated to all the children in our family, especially Frances, who is our most candid and formative assessor.

Acknowledgements

The authors and publishers would like to thank the following for permission to reproduce material:

The Controller of Her Majesty's Stationery Office for the extracts on pages 8, 12, 81 and 92.

Croom Helm Publishers for the chart on page 80.

The Daily Telegraph for the extract on page 6.

Helen F. Hadley of Kenyngton Manor First and Middle School for the hand-on forms on page 30.

Hodder & Stoughton, Publishers, for the diagnostic tests on page 36.

The Independent for the extract on page 6.

The National Curriculum Council, York, for the leaflet on page 9.

The Observer for the extract on page 6.

The School Examinations & Assessment Council for the extracts on pages 8 and 35.

About this book

Chapter 1 addresses the concerns which provoked the introduction of a National Curriculum and its accompanying assessment arrangements. It contains discussion about what the law now demands and critical comment on some of the official document-ation related to assessment. We have also tried to elaborate on current practice in schools. Then we can all endeavour to marry what is 'good' in assessment practice with what we are obliged to do to comply with the law.

Chapter 2 is the 'agony aunt' chapter. It is all about resolving worries and concerns so that you can become an expert assessor. It consists of a number of situations against which you match your own feelings and opinions. Each one presents exemplar material about over-coming difficulties and achieving some common understanding about what we are assessing and how to do it.

Chapter 3 describes and explains the vocab-ulary of assessment by looking in detail at many of the main technical words and devices in common use today. They have come from the natural sciences, statistics, sociology and other sources. They are words which have been adopted within the assessment field because they are useful. Some of these technical terms can be confusing. We have all found in print, and heard in voiced opinions, ideas that show that people abuse statistics. So too do they misuse technical terms by, for example, referring to the results of tests without knowing how they are arrived at or what they mean, confusing validity and reliability, and talking about objective class-room research. An understanding of the terms not only enables us to evaluate what we read and what we hear, but also helps us to become skilled users of these ideas ourselves.

Chapter 4 is conceptually and actually pivotal to the book both in terms of ideas and content. In it we look at what it is that children do in school that is available for assessment, and the techniques teachers can use to assess what children do. These techniques include formal and informal methods. None of the techniques are 'brand new' and all teachers will have employed some of them from time to time. Our hope is that, in describing them in detail, we will increase your expertise in areas that you have not found to be your métier. You will also be able to systematize and streamline your methods with conviction. There are also examples to show how assessment can be carried through.

Chapter 5 is all about communication. Even if you are an expert on the assessment of children in school, your findings will be entirely useless unless you can communicate them to the audience for whom they are intended (including yourself!). That gem of observation you scribbled down last month may not look quite so insightful now, unless, that is, you have translated it into something that still makes sense. We cover the spread of possible assessments, ranging from the impression of a moment to the sight of a test result, and from the systematic recording of observations over time to the creation of composite grades from a list of judgements and marks. The intention, in this chapter, is to help you develop a range of meaningful records of assessment.

Chapter 6 brings together the 'why', 'what', 'how' and 'who for' of assessment. All this expertise has to be matched with considerable management skills for assessment to be carried out in school. Assessment has to be an every day, every way activity; firstly, just because it is a continual aspect of classroom life and secondly, because if assessments are to fuel the future, that applies as much to tomorrow as to next term; what you do on Monday affects what you do on Tuesday. The SEAC endorse this by referring to teacher assessment as:

> ❝*of a moving picture; if the action taken on the basis of the assessment is effective, the original information is soon out of date. . .*❞
> *A Guide to Teacher Assessment,* Pack C, A Source Book of Teacher Assessment (SEAC, 1990)1.4, p. 6

The teacher's classroom management has to be geared to daily change on the basis of informed judgements or assessments. It is vital that this is seen in the context of whole-school plans.

Chapter 7 takes you on from amassing the techniques and the management skills to working out your own individual action list and style. You can still carry out assessment as you wish, and make the research approaches your own, enhancing your curriculum vitae and adding to your portfolio of professional skills.

This book has no sections, because it can be read and used from beginning to end in linear fashion. However, you may prefer to start by reflecting on Chapters 1 and 2; then you can look for ideas for your own action list in Chapter 7. You can then dip into and use information from Chapters 3, 4, 5 and 6 when you need to.

Introduction

MOST IMAGINATIVE   TALLEST   MOST COLOURFUL

Assessment: A natural thing to do

We all try to make judgements about our own learning and that of other people of all ages. We may tell a neighbour how pretty his or her garden is looking, comment on new recipes tried at home, and we may ask our friends how their evening classes are coming along. We may say to our children, 'How was school today?' or to a nephew, 'What is your best subject?' Bits of information like this fuel our daily assessments. Some people would identify this need to compare and categorise individuals as 'human nature'.

What we regard as part of 'human nature' profoundly affects our views about education. It is a common assumption that people are motivated solely by competition, and this affects our views on testing. Some of us may make specific judgements about individuals on the basis of their 'nature': i.e. the skills and traits they are assumed to have inherited. Other people would perhaps claim that whilst there are some basic human traits, it is the environment in which youngsters grow up that is of major importance. These people may also identify co-operation as being more important for personal development than competition. Differing and sometimes polarised views on these issues are often referred to as the debate about 'nature versus nurture'.

Nature versus nurture

In the 'nature versus nurture' debate the issue is whether innate ability predominates or whether the environment has the major impact on a child's educational performance. Up until the turn of the twentieth century, the prevailing ethos in education seems to have been on the 'nature' side of the argument. Much of the groundwork and many of the traditions in our assessment and examination systems were established before 'nurture' began to receive public attention.

Emphasising heredity   Many people believe that just as we inherit a certain number of toes and the colour of our eyes, we also inherit other characteristics, including the ability to take initiatives and make responses in our learning. They also believe that the degree to which we can do well in school is limited by our inherited abilities. The argument goes that what is inherited is immutable. Our potential is thus limited by our physiological and intellectual inheritance, and at best the teacher can effect only marginal changes in capacity to learn. The role of the teacher is to ensure that children learn to the maximum of their given capability. Closely associated with this view is the belief that environmental conditions are the product of the abilities of those living in those conditions. People with limited ability create limited home environments. People with greater ability offer broader, more extended environmental experiences and opportunities. These views have been very influential in a number of educational initiatives and policy decisions. They are also clearly related to tests and methods of testing. Of particular influence was the work of Burt and others on the construction and refinement of intelligence

1

tests. The latter were put to educational use in the tripartite system of secondary education and formed the backbone of the 11+ examination.

Emphasising the environment To take an environmental view is to accept that children are born without strong predetermined limits to their intellectual development. The effect of educative experience on children is to increase their capabilities. The work of, for example, Froebel and Montessori represents the environmental view. They propounded ideas in support of child-centred education and adopted a long-term developmental approach, starting at birth. They saw that the limits on development depended on the quality of experience offered by parents and teachers. Montessori, for example, worked on producing resources through which children could learn independently. Toys currently in the shops, such as the doll with a buckle, lace, button and zip are commercial attempts at emulating her ideas in practice. A.S. Neill, the founder of Summerhill, is among the best-known educationalists in this tradition. If the focus is exclusively on environmental enhancement for developing individuals, then assessment through comparison with other children ceases to be valid.

This long-standing academic debate still goes on, and has a profound effect on our current attitudes to assessment, and on educational legislation.

Assessment of schoolchildren

Parents and teachers make assessments concerning the children in their care. They want those children to improve their repertoire of skills and increase their store of knowledge. These concerned adults also want to have some external estimation of how well the children are doing from time to time. The roots of formal assessment lie in such needs. Indeed, to a certain extent the whole schooling system is based on the notion of measured achievement linked to chronological age. Traditionally children are assessed formally at certain ages, rather than at points in their individual development. This is one way in which our day-to-day experience differs from formal assessments. We do not always judge the garden on the age of the gardener!

As the welter of things that can be assessed has increased, so there has developed a growing realisation that there is more to assessment in school than everyday impressions. Teachers know this. Their experience tells them that assessing human achievement and potential is a tricky, time-consuming and arduous business.

How teachers view assessment

Good teachers have always tried to assess their pupils' work. They have done so because it is the teacher's own assessments which fuel his or her planning and his or her teaching. These judgements inform teachers about the appropriateness and the presentation of the subject they are teaching. They tell them what the children have learned, and indicate the children's capacity to learn more, thus pointing the direction of future teaching. How else can you know whether teaching and learning is progressing as you would wish, except by making assessments and evaluations along the way?

Teachers already make informed judgements about their own teaching and children's learning every day, and use assessment information to good effect. Despite this, the imposition of the external National Curriculum assessment demands seems to have had an adverse effect on teachers. It has made some teachers begin to lose sight of the efficacy of carrying out assessment, and to lose confidence in the expertise they already have. The climate in some schools is one of anxiety, stress and a feeling of oppression.

National assessment and teachers   We think that the manner of the introduction of the National Curriculum package is an affront to the teaching profession. Such sweeping changes demand the whole-hearted support of teachers if they are to be successful. Detailed planning is also required for effective delivery. It does seem to us that the timetable for implementation has been one of indecent haste, and one which puts pressure on an already beleaguered profession. These arguments also apply to the assessment arrangements.

However, the demand that the Government abandon the idea of national assessment entirely is, in our view, counter-productive. The system, as originally envisaged, may well turn out to be unmanageable. Even if that is the case, assessment will still be an important aspect of the work of every teacher. It is therefore to our own advantage to put our energies into fully understanding assessment systems and their implications, and to be ready to use creatively those assessment strategies we know work in the best interests of children. Teachers can then develop and refine assessment so that it commands the respect of outsiders as a demanding, sophisticated and skilful part of their job. In other words, teachers can make what they have always done, that is use assessment to fuel their teaching, into a pivotal area of professional expertise. What is different now, is that this expertise is much more open to public scrutiny than hitherto.

Teachers as expert assessors   With planning and organisation, teachers can adopt a professional, well-articulated attitude to assessment, seeing it as an integral component of

their teaching and children's learning. People who are not teachers not only lack a full understanding of how assessment is done, but also have only a limited grasp of what it is for. Examinations and tests are very much part of the indelible childhood memory of every adult. Whether they attended an exclusive public school or the local comprehensive, the majority of people, from legislator to man in the street, probably think of assessment as a grim ordeal where many suffer the ignominy of failure. Most assessments that teachers are now able to do are not of that kind at all. Teachers have to change the climate of opinion from a position where we understand only 'pass' or 'fail' to one where we start to talk about 'next steps', 'future possibilities' and 'potential'. To spread these ideas, it will be necessary for teachers to explain the purposes, strengths and weaknesses and interpretation of assessments.

However, the balance of assessments as originally envisaged under the National Curriculum would not entirely assist the possibilities for broad, forward-looking assessments. In tackling the issue of national assessment, the Task Group On Assessment and Testing published a report suggesting that formal tests should not be all-important. Whilst taking these suggestions on board, the School Examinations and Assessment Council made recommendations that Standard Assessment Task (SAT) results, where available, should have precedence over Teacher Assessments (TA). The spectre of national formal testing of primary children was raised. However, as SATs and tests are being tried out, there is a growing realisation that it is essential to place a high proportion of assessment in the hands of teachers, to make the operation more manageable. Some may see this as a face-saving way of making teachers and local authorities responsible for assessment delivery, thereby shifting the locus for any problems that arise. There are also, however, clear opportunities for teachers to assert the central importance of the progress and potential of each and every child in their care, not just classes, cohorts or year groups as a whole. If teachers are permitted to make judgements which are open to review by their peers, choosing, when necessary, from a large bank of test materials produced through rigorous trialling, then we have every chance of developing an assessment system which will further enhance teachers' competence and the realisation of children's potential.

The task ahead

There is to be a period of several years of piloting, adjustment and modification before the National Curriculum assessment arrangements can be said to be in place. That does give teachers the opportunity to experiment with and devise ways of marrying external demands with their own preferred ways of working. In implementing what are seen by some people as additional chores, teachers still have control. There is no insistence that professional expertise in teaching and learning should be subordinated to the assessment giant and the test ogre. We need to make them assist education, and not control it.

To do this it is necessary for all of us working in the education system to take stock of our knowledge of and views on the following:

- The impact of 'nature' vis-à-vis 'nurture'
- Assessment techniques and approaches
- The extent to which we can influence educational potential.

If we use assessment to enhance change, growth and development, rather than to encourage labelling and compartmentalising, all the children in our care will reap the benefit. Whilst assessment is the servant of curriculum, it can also be the key to ensuring an enthralling and apposite curriculum for every child. We do, however, need to dissect the current legislation to determine how far it assists this endeavour. Thus Chapter 1 focuses on the disquiet which provoked the establishment of a National Curriculum and its assessment arrangements, what the emergent legislation contains, and how far this marries with what teachers currently do.

1

on the mat?

NATIONAL CURRICULUM ASSESSMENT

The reasons for national measures

Two of the main purposes behind the National Curriculum which have important implications for assessment are:

- To raise standards
- To improve performance in scientific and technological areas.

There is in fact nothing new in this, for a similar desire was expressed at the Great Exhibition of 1851 and again at the Festival of Britain in 1951! What is different now, perhaps, is that we do not seem to be at the threshold of an expansive new era for Britain; rather there is concern about the economic future of the nation. The National Curriculum is one of the important responses to these concerns. 'Standards' and 'performance' will be central to appraisals and evaluations of the success of the National Curriculum in years to come.

This means that the efficacy of the assessment arrangements following the National Curriculum prescriptions will test out whether the legislation meets current concerns. Assessment is pivotal, for there will be no way of judging the effectiveness of the legislation in its entirety, except by some kind of assessment made available outside the school.

Standards

In order to raise standards there are two major prerequisites. They are:

- To articulate desired standards
- To identify existing standards.

Desired standards   The National Curriculum working parties have been given the brief of defining the knowledge, skills and understanding that children need. The approach to this task is characterised by the use of subject labels. The model employed is 'top down'. In other words, the statements of attainment and the programmes of study have, in the main, been produced by establishing the level which children should ideally have reached (i.e. key stage 4), and then the formal curriculum has been defined in terms of the steps (i.e. levels) through which children need to progress in order to achieve that ambition.

Existing standards   Much of the impetus to raise existing standards has come from impressions rather than hard data. There is a feeling that the schooling system has not 'come up with the goods', and there are repeated reports in the Press concerning the extent to which Britain lags behind other countries in terms of educational achievement.

THE DAILY TELEGRAPH, FRIDAY, AUGUST 31, 1990

Only tougher testing can halt this classroom rot

FERDINAND MOUNT

©Daily Telegraph plc

THE INDEPENDENT Thursday 8 February 1990

At the bottom of the class

By Peter Jenkins

Something on a grand scale is required if Britain is to avoid the humiliation of continuing decline. . . . a profound change in attitudes is needed if Britain is to cease to be the most ill-educated nation in the developed world.

OBSERVER 26 August 1990

Learn lessons of schools for scandal

Barry Hugill, our Education Correspondent, shares Sir Claus Moser's alarm at declining standards.

It is very difficult to judge the effectiveness, or otherwise, of a school system. Sir Claus chose the staying-on rate: the number of youngsters who stay on at school or go full-time to college. In the UK it is 35 per cent, in the USA 79 per cent, in Japan 77 per cent, and in Sweden 76 per cent.

We can argue that the odds are stacked against our primary schools, for they have the lowest capitation in the system, low status, low profile in terms of discussion of 'success' and so on. If we face up to the adverse comments and prejudices of recent times, we can do much to redress misconceptions and meet criticisms. In order to do so there is a need to open up assessment discussions and use the National Curriculum as a device for promoting the professional image of the teacher in the primary school. Possible outcomes include:

- The furthering of public understanding of the special demands of work in primary schools
- The development of an appreciation of the unique contributions made to children's educative experiences by good primary teachers.

A major factor in ensuring these outcomes is going to be teachers' competent and sensitive handling of the assessment demands made on them.

Performance in science and technology

With the intention of improving Britain's performance in scientific and technological areas, the compilers of the National Curriculum documents and the accompanying assessment arrangements have tried to bring about a major shift of content and emphasis in what is done in schools. To do this they have placed science at the core of the curriculum, and have identified technology as one of the foundation subjects. To make science (in contrast to 'nature study', or even physics, chemistry and biology) a subject at the heart of the curriculum, to be studied and assessed until everyone is 16, is a step without precedent in our educational history. Technology is a subject of recent identification, and it is a mark of its anticipated importance that it should reach all children, particularly those in infant schools.

A fresh start to assessment?

The introduction of the National Curriculum and associated assessment arrangements does not mean that we can assume that we teachers are starting things anew or even afresh. We all carry with us views on the nature of children, priorities about what is important learning, and ideas about the means of assessment and associated outcomes. These views come from our own educational experiences as well as from popular perceptions.

Everyone in education is committed to analysis, reflection and change. We do, however, need to understand where we are now, in order to meet current and future assessment expectations more efficiently. We need to take account of three important sets of issues:

● Assessment systems already in schools
● Assessment requirements of the National Curriculum
● Assessment in practice.

Assessment systems in use

The assessments of children currently made in schools are products of the ideas provoked by the 'heredity versus environment' debate, the ways in which the curriculum is described, and the implementation of legislation. The outcomes of the interplay of all these factors has left us with a legacy of anomalies to contend with. These include problems such as which kinds of tests to use, how to balance formal and informal assessment, and whether formative or summative assessment is to be

the greater part of the teacher's role. Whilst these issues are addressed in later chapters of this book, it is important to focus here on the kinds of assessment systems and structures already established in schools. The National Curriculum is not only concerned with content; it also has an important effect on the ways in which we must view the provision of learning opportunities in the different sectors of education.

The primary sector

Following in the wake of the general demise of the 11+, and the gradual permeation of child-centred educational ideas into schools, many teachers have moved away from assessment which is tied solely to academic achievement. There is now a concern for the development of the whole child. It has become common for teachers of young children to comment not only on their academic achievement, but also on their maturity, attention and concentration skills, ability to organise their own learning and so on. In order to accommodate this change in emphasis and broaden the assessment spectrum, some forms of school record have expanded the 'open' comments boxes for these kinds of assessments and judgements.

The secondary sector

Because the secondary sector is more strongly governed by examinations, external formal assessment has been central to secondary practice. Over recent years, however, there have been pressures from outside education on secondary schools. These pressures have encouraged moves to make assessment reflect more than just examination performance. The political climate and job shortages facing the school-leaver have, together with developments such as the Technical and Vocational Education Initiative, focused the attention of many secondary teachers on the preparation of their pupils for a job search. Secondary schools are increasingly providing young people with personal profiles which set out assessments regarding social and personal skills, in addition to academic ones. Employers too, have begun to emphasise that oracy, personal presentation and social skills are important for successful interview technique and achieving confidence and success in work. The profiling trend in the secondary sector has gathered momentum, and will inevitably lead to the promotion of profiling approaches in feeder schools.

National curriculum assessment requirements

The Education Reform Act

The law is unequivocal about what teachers should assess. In the words of the Education Reform Act, in each of the core and other foundation subjects:

> "*at or near the end of each key stage . . . ascertain what (pupils) have achieved in relation to the attainment targets for that stage.*"
>
> *A Guide to Teacher Assessment, Pack C, A Source Book of Teacher Assessment (SEAC, 1990) part 1.2 (c)*

Other official advice endorses the idea that assessment is about what children know and can do. Information from the School Examinations and Assessment Council (SEAC) is as follows:

> "*Assessment in the context of the National Curriculum relates to achievement. It does not relate to attitude or personality.*"
>
> ibid. 2.8, p. 15

The Act also says that:

> "*'assess' includes examine and test*"
>
> ibid. part 1.16 (1)

Additions to minimum requirements

DES regulations   If the words of the ERA were the only guidance teachers had about the content of assessment, then much of the experience gained over the last two decades would be lost. However, DES regulations regarding school records present a slightly different, and more contemporary picture. In the regulations there is talk of:

> "*academic achievements, other skills and abilities and progress in school*"
>
> *The Education (School Records) Regulations 1989 (DES) Circular No. 17/89, para. 5*

The point is also made that some schools keep information in excess of that required by regulation, including, for example, details about attendance, emotional development and home background. It says:

> "*Many schools find such information indispensable in building up a full picture of the pupil, and thus in promoting educational attainment and good behaviour.*"
>
> ibid. para. 17

Profiles of achievement   National Curriculum assessment does dictate that, at a minimum, teachers should undertake the assessment of achievement at the ends of key stages. This minimum requirement could lead to a reduction in the kinds of assessments carried out. However, we believe it unlikely that schools will revert to earlier practices in which assessment was entirely geared to testing and the reporting of test results. The regulations for annual reports to be made to parents should also, perversely, help to add weight to assessments that are broader than marks, grades and scores. (See *Records of Achievement* (DES) Circular No. 8/90. There is also more detail about this in Chapter 5). The benefits to children, parents and teachers, of more complete profiles of achievement and potential are now clear to many people, and the demand for sophisticated information will increase, not diminish. In other words it will not suffice to reduce children's learning to a tick next to levels or profile components. This does, of course, leave the problem of exactly what else to include. There is more discussion of these issues in Chapter 5. In order to develop a satisfactory response to the demands of assessment within the National Curriculum it is necessary to identify both what is feasible and what is appropriate.

Understanding assessment documentation

Since the Education Reform Act was passed, schools have been inundated with reports, information and advice about the National Curriculum. These have come from many sources. The range of comment and advice on assessment has, if anything, been even wider because assessment issues concern a broader range of people. There have been attempts in the Press to inform parents, some trying to educate, others overemphasising aspects of the legislation. There have been discussions about the politics of assessment, with the result that responsibility for key stage 1 and 2 assessment has been handed over to local authorities. There have also been public battles over the content of some subjects, and teaching unions have made statements about the burden of the paperwork in assessment and the stress it is causing members of the teaching profession.

We have put to one side the reactions and comment in the Press. This does not mean that they are unimportant, for they may significantly influence public opinion, and that includes the parents of the children you

Part of a free pamphlet for parents, informing them about the National Curriculum
Reproduced by permission of the National Curriculum Council, York

9

teach. There is, however, considerable evidence which would suggest that the parents you know will try to form opinions about you as an individual, quite apart from any general feelings they may have about standards, assessment or any other educational issue. Your credibility depends not on press reports, but on how well you translate the legislation into practice for the particular children in your care. The documents we shall focus on, in addition to the Statutory Orders related to assessment, are the publications produced by SEAC to assist teachers.

SEAC publications

The SEAC booklets *A Guide to Teacher Assessment: Packs A, B and C* (1990) predate the Statutory Orders by some months. The intention has been to produce a distance learning package geared to helping teachers to be evaluators. That is an appropriate and timely idea, although the structure, format and introductory information does not make clear that intention. It is worthwhile reviewing these booklets critically, for we feel there are some serious flaws in these SEAC publications. Here are our views:

- Learning packs do need to take account of needs of the learner *in context*. These are not materials for learners in any field which teachers might light upon and adapt. They were written specifically *for* teachers. Why then are the exercises demanded so impractical?
- Learning packs benefit from attractive presentation and layout, but if the sense is sacrificed for heading size, lettering and numbering, this makes successful learning more difficult.
- Models are useful in presenting and linking ideas concisely, but only if they make sense when applied.

- When reading these booklets we are forced to apply too narrow a frame of reference. It is as though they are the work of a limited number of people, and there is little chance to say, 'I do not see it like that – is there another way it can be done?'
- Teacher assessment is important and serious. The SEAC booklets are dangerously near to being too slick. This could lead to suggestions which demean teachers' skills.

Nevertheless, please do not reject the SEAC booklets out of hand, or in the light of our criticisms. They are there to be challenged, but also to be put to use. With all your critical faculties on hand, go ahead and 'choose and use'.

The Statutory Orders

The Statutory Orders are open to creative interpretation, but not rejection. You must understand and implement them. The draft Statutory Orders regarding assessment of key stage 1 English, mathematics and science were published in May 1990. The main recommendations are shown opposite.

These recommendations will be determined by SATs, where applicable, and by TA in all other cases. (There is more discussion of documentation related to reports in Chapter 5.)

Special provisions   For pupils for whom part of the National Curriculum does not apply, the rules on profile component level and subject level can be modified. There are also some special arrangements for dealing with children's absence. For children whose first language is not English there are also some indications as to what is allowable.

Monitoring   This is the responsibility of the LEAs. They have to ensure their schools'

ASSESSMENT OF CHILDREN AT THE END OF THE KEY STAGE

By end of spring term (or March 31 if that is later):

- TAs, defining levels of attainment reached in each AT put in summary record

By end of first half of summer term:

- SATs to be done
- Assessment based on SATs completed

RECORDS OF ASSESSMENT

Records of assessment comprise:

- TAs of attainment in all applicable attainment targets
- Level of attainment in each attainment target covered by a SAT
- SATs performance levels to take precedence over TA where available (except where a profile component will be affected)

The following also apply:

Profile Components

- Profile component level is the highest level in half or more of the attainment targets (except in writing, where the PC is the level for writing or the higher of the levels reached in spelling and handwriting, where they are lower than writing)

Subject scores

- Subject score is the average of the PC levels (to the nearest whole number)
  English and science PCs have equal weighting
  Mathematics PCs are weighted: Number, algebra and measures 3, Shape and space and data handling 2

REPORTS

For each National Curriculum subject, reports should include the level of attainment in:

- The subject as a whole
- Each profile component
- Each attainment target (this record may be supplied to parents on request, or at the school's discretion, without request).

assessments are consistent with national standards, and sort out discrepancies between TAs and SATs results where teachers think the latter are unrealistic. They also have to arrange assessment INSET (Inservice Education and Training of Teachers).

Timing The first national assessments at the end of key stage 1 take place in 1991, and at the end of key stage 2 in 1994. From these dates individual children's results will go to their parents. Aggregated statistics on key stage 2 levels of attainment will be made public from 1995 onwards. There is no legal requirement to publish results at the end of key stage 1.

Critique of the Statutory Orders

Key stage 1 external assessments have now been confined to the core subjects of English, mathematics and science. They have literally been pared to the core! It is ironic that, though teachers decry the need for external assessment, problems arise when they are asked to do 'tests' in only part of the curriculum and not all of it. The limited coverage of assessment prescriptions may actually provoke some teachers to focus on those things they have to assess, to the exclusion of other subjects. We then have a narrowing of the curriculum as experienced by some children in school.

The legislation is confined to setting up what is called 'a broad framework' for along-the-way assessment. It is difficult to see what this framework comprises. At the ends of key stages the directives are quite specific and detailed. There is a problem in this approach. On the one hand, we would applaud the idea that teachers, schools and groups of schools should be given considerable freedom in devising their own records for children during the key stages. On the other hand, it is likely that detailed requirements at the ends of phases of education will lead to an increased emphasis on these *summative* assessments, at the expense of the *formative* assessments made throughout the child's career.

However, if as is recommended the administration of SATs is placed in the hands of classteachers, the head along with his or her whole staff will have to determine what can be done to facilitate the work of those teachers doing assessment. Not only will classteachers need extra help at the time when SATs are being done, but they will need support to complete the necessary compilation and reporting of

assessments. There does not seem to be much extra funding given directly to schools to cover this.

Time to take heart:

> **"**the Secretary of State has endorsed SEAC's advice that . . . the actual conduct and delivery of assessments and the determination of outcomes is for primary schools.**"**
>
> Draft: *The Education Reform Act 1988:* National Curriculum: Order under Section 4 for Assessment Arrangements in English, mathematics and science at key stage 1, May 1990

This is a very important point. It is so for two reasons: firstly, it places the most important part of the whole business firmly in the hands of classteachers. It is *your* judgements that will carry the day. The children's futures are in your hands. Secondly, it may be possible, now that schools are responsible for financial decisions, to buy in help during the latter half of the spring term each year to provide additional assistance for the teacher doing SATs.

Help in understanding assessment documentation

If you find the documentation incomprehensible, ask for help! Teachers, who are just the people to advise learners about what to do when they get stuck, are reluctant to carry through their own advice! You will need the help of your colleagues to carry through assessment anyway, so why not enlist their help at the outset? Ask the headteacher or assessment co-ordinator to help you. Schools are being encouraged to set up their own INSET on assessment. If the meetings or speakers do not prove helpful, say so! If there is no one in school to whom you may turn for guidance, approach the advisory team. Their role is, or has been, to be available to help teachers. In those authorities where the advisory role has been substituted for an inspectorial role, approaches may be more difficult. If there is a teacher training establishment near to you then do make contact. They will only be too happy to try to give support and advice.

The benefits of national assessment now

The current assessment picture in many schools is characterised by the notion of individual progress. Underlying this is a set of beliefs about growth and potential for those individuals. There is an increased use of broad and varied reporting procedures and many teachers are committed to offering more than literal grades to describe children and their personal achievements. Whilst there is still a central concern for formal examination success, there is also a clear appreciation of the need for young people to leave the formal school system at 16 years of age with more than just a set of certificates. It is in this setting that National Curriculum assessment has to operate. Despite the problems of implementing a national system, it has two possible positive benefits for teachers:

- It supports and furthers good practice (i.e. it is useful to teachers)
- It supports children's learning.

Assessment in practice

The teacher

'Current' and 'good' practice Having supported the importance of assessment for teaching and learning, it is unfortunate that much of what has been written about assessment under the National Curriculum is rather patronising of teachers. There seems to be a lack of recognition of the experience of primary teachers in the assessment field. There is also an assumption that, since the general disappearance of the 11+, there has been little or no assessment in primary schools. Whilst few teachers in primary schools would claim to be 'experts' on assessment, there is an abundance of appropriate expertise in this sector. The fact that primary teachers have actually been in the vanguard of such things as open learning, team teaching and profiling of the achievements of individuals, is often overlooked. These are all developments which may feature in even more schools as they adapt to the demands of the National Curriculum.

For the primary school teacher, there is really nothing new being said about assessment. There are no new techniques being invented, and no special or different tasks to do. Teachers already observe children, note the occurrence of conceptual leaps, compile class plans and complete individual records including statements of performance and future needs.

Teachers are commonly appraised against 'good practice'. The many definitions of good practice are derived from the perspectives of these three main groups:

- HMI
- Teacher educators and advisers
- Interested people, for example, parents and politicians, and others outside the education professions.

Given the range of possible views it is not surprising that there are, at times, contradictory messages about what is 'good' in the field of assessment. There are pressures on the one hand for external, quantifiable and generalised accountability, and on the other, for individualised, formative, and qualitative progression. Teachers must operate to satisfy both these sets of demands in assessing their pupils. To do so requires planning and management of learning and the evaluation of teaching and its outcomes.

Planning and management of learning In the SEAC documents on assessment three typical models of classroom organisation are mentioned:

- Children placed in three or four ability groups, all working in same subject area, with teacher starting off the whole class and then spreading his or her attention between groups and individuals
- Children placed in three or four groups, each group working on a different curriculum area, with teacher focusing on one group and nominally supervising the others
- Children working on activities they have chosen themselves, with teacher supporting individuals.

The SEAC then say that each of these typical situations offers opportunities for assessment. From the descriptions there follow a number of expectations about what will happen in classrooms. Teachers are going to have to embrace mixed modes of organisation. At times the concentration will be on teaching the whole class; at other times on the provision of opportunities for groups of children to be working on different tasks. The brief of the SEAC does not include prescriptions about class organisation but the examples they have chosen make it clear that there is no support for class teaching as a permanent or even 'majority of the time' approach.

It seems likely that only by a flexible grouping situation will teachers have the chance to collect all the assessment information they require. There are possibilities for individual teachers to match the kind of grouping they set up with the kind of learning they are about to assess. It will be through his or her own evaluations of match between organisation, kind of learning to be assessed and how he or she is to do the assessing, that each teacher will become an ever more skilled manager of learning.

Evaluation of teaching Complementing the skills of learning manager are those of teacher. It is easy to forget, amongst the mass of management information, that the main part of a teacher's job is to teach! 'Good practice' in teaching depends upon informed intervention, stimulating lessons, and the repeated but varied presentation of ideas. Much of the good work of teachers is actually quite hard to describe in a logical way. There is still an important intuitive element built into the teacher-child relationship. However, through constant and continuous assessment of teaching and learning, teachers can modify and adjust their own teaching plans and strategies to optimise children's progress. But to do so does need the support of analysis.

The major factors in classroom teaching are the child, the teacher and the content of teaching episodes. This triangle of inter-related factors is held in balance by the teacher. Formal assessment alone, and allegiance to prescribed content will unbalance the triangle. The evaluation of classroom processes and practice, and particularly teaching, is an essential co-requisite of any assessment system, along with continuing studies of what is being learned.

Change in practice What the Education Reform Act does make mandatory, and for some teachers this will mean a change in the balance of what they and the children in their care do in a school day, is that detailed and piecemeal recording must be done specifically related to levels of attainment in attainment targets within the foundation subjects. This means that teachers will have to complete tables and charts which are internally consistent within a school, and may vary little between schools. To make sure records and all that leads up to them are meaningful for teachers and children, there will need to be active sharing of good practice within and across schools.

The children

All too often assessment is viewed as a summation of what is already past. There are two reasons why we cannot justify assessment of children as measures only of past achievement:

- The labelling of children as failures is destructive and serves no purpose
- With very little more work, assessments can be made to serve the future as well as providing intermediate résumés of achievement, and this is both more cost-effective and more positive.

National Curriculum assessment will not restrict children's futures if teachers do not allow it to. Through engaging children in the construction of the path of their own learning, teachers will further enhance two aspects of education. They will help children to see learning as a continuous process in which they themselves can help to overcome sticking points and setbacks. They will also help children to become self-determining learners who can steer their own course through the material provided and beyond. We often see complaints about young people which suggest that they are lazy and unwilling to learn. Rather than respond to these sorts of opinions by tightening assessments, we would urge that children should be given the kinds of educative experience which motivate them to succeed and promote the emergence of flexible and responsible adults. Education really is the only way to create a diverse yet mutually respectful society. In setting up classroom experiences for children, it is useful to reflect on the models of learning that we are operating.

How children learn   It would take a whole book to sum up the current thinking on the ways children learn. There are in common usage at least two main schools of thought.

Put very simply, these two perspectives may be summarised as follows:

- Learners respond to the stimulus of new learning when offered a reward. This could be a tick, a mark, praise, a gold star or an exam grade. There is often an assumption that what happens within the child is not important. These kinds of ideas are supported by behavioural psychologists.
- Learners are constantly adding to and refining their cognitive 'map' of their world. The motivation is a search for meaning, and with more learning comes more sophisticated understanding. The emphases here are on what individuals think and know. People working in these fields are sometimes referred to as cognitive theorists.

As teachers we are eclectic, and adopt one or the other of these two perspectives according to our own predilections and to the kind of learning we are engaged in. When we have taught a child how to hold a pencil or throw a ball, we may have employed a behaviourist model: offering praise, breaking the learning down into small steps and taking the child through the routine of steps. When we have taught a child how to write a letter of complaint we may employ a cognitive model, and expect the child to compose a letter containing his or her own views about the issue. It is important to note that either approach can be taken to any kind of learning. Each approach carries a number of assumptions and a different conceptual vocabulary. We can simply use whichever seems more appropriate.

A common way of tackling children's learning, which bypasses how it actually happens but employs some elements of both a behaviourist and a cognitive approach, is to identify what it is that children who are good at something can actually do, and then give learners the experience of all those kinds of tasks. We sometimes tackle the teaching of reading, writing and maths like this. For example, in reading we show children how we get meaning from the squiggles on a page and not just from the pictures; we show them that we start at the top left-hand corner and that we read from left to right; we let them see that we enjoy reading and that reading lets us into other worlds of the not-here-and-not-now. Competent readers would say 'of course' to all of this, and most would not be able to say whether, with a particular book, it was the reward of teacher's smile or the fun of finding out whether the story ended in the way they hoped that helped them to get to the last page.

The model of learning we employ does have some effect on the approach to assessment we may adopt. The links between a behaviourist view and formal tests are readily made. Cognitive explanations mean a broader approach, using skills other than those of the scientist to determine the meaning of outcomes. In addition to mixed patterns of classroom organisation, a variety of ways of presenting tasks and mixed strategies for conceptualising children's learning will help teachers most in planning the teaching, learning and assessment of the whole curriculum.

Summary

In many respects assessment is the greatest asset and also the biggest bugbear in teaching. On the one hand it is a pleasure to be able to point to successful learning through assessment; on the other hand the tools of assessment can threaten to be reductionist and crude. As teachers we have a major responsibility for the operation of the assessment of children now. The judgements we make, whether with the aid of 'tests' or not, can offer possibilities for intellectual growth or, if we are not careful, stunt that growth.

In this chapter we have said that we work in an education system where there is a tradition of mixed styles of assessment. We have primary schools which emphasise individual development whilst comparing one group with another; we administer formal tests whilst building individual profiles of personal achievement; we accept that some children are more or less able than others whilst setting universal attainment targets. It is, then, in a system of contradictions, which will hopefully lead to a creative tension, that we have to operate the national assessment of young children. We hope that teachers choose to harness the benefits of *having to* assess in the cause of better planning and management for themselves, and of increased future learning opportunities for the children in their care.

So what is new? We are expected to do our best, and that will only come out of informed action. For that informed action, we need to:

- Overcome our fears and prejudices about doing assessment
- Know about the technical terms in assessment
- Distinguish between the kinds of things we are assessing
- Perfect the skills necessary to being an assessor
- Refine ways of acting on assessment outcomes
- Manage assessment strategies in schools and classrooms.

The chapters that follow develop each of these aspects in turn.

2

OVERCOMING OBSTACLES TO ASSESSMENT

Below are some of the comments about National Curriculum assessment that we have heard, seen in the Press, or which we regard as typical. They all constitute barriers to 'getting on with the job'. They have not all come from individual classroom teachers but we have phrased them so, because teachers themselves do need to get to grips with the problems within the context of the school in which they work. We have organised them under a set of headings which represent areas of concern about assessment.

Tests and testing

" I am antipathetic to the idea of testing small children."

" The children I teach do not have sufficient skills to approach tests."

Pressure from parents and friends

" The children I teach are already under tremendous pressure from their parents to excel. I do not want to add to their anxiety."

"I fear the higher profile of assessment will adversely affect the way children view one another."

Assessment management

" I think 'official' assessment takes up valuable teaching time."

" There is too much to assess. I think children's progress can be monitored without blanket coverage."

What to assess

"I find it hard to sort out exactly what it is that I am assessing."

"I am not sure how to handle children's 'performances', especially in 'one-off' test situations."

Assessment records

> " I am no good at keeping tidy detailed records of assessment."
>
> "I find it difficult to fit my insights onto forms that I have not devised."

Assessment expertise

> "I do not feel I have the breadth of experience yet to make categorical judgements about individual children"

In some schools the support of colleagues, management strategies and INSET will contribute to the satisfactory solution of the dilemmas raised. In others individual teachers may feel they lack support in sorting out their concerns. To carry through assessment realistically and meaningfully demands profound understanding of what you are doing and positive commitment to seeing it through. The intention here is to help remove obstacles to that commitment.

We shall look at each of these dilemmas in turn. For each we shall try, through anecdote and case-study material, to identify the main elements in the problem, discuss possible ways of approaching them and some of the likely outcomes. Inevitably we make reference to other parts of the book, but not where it will detract from the thread of the argument.

No to tests

This is the heart of the matter, and you may find that many of your colleagues agree with you. It could be argued that our education system rests on a form of elitism where competitive examinations dominate. There is an idea that children should 'get used to' such competition, and the younger they do so the better. We would reject that kind of argument and resist the labelling of children as being of one calibre or another on the basis of test results. Overemphasis on what children can or cannot do *now* closes future options, and we firmly believe there is untapped potential in everybody. However, there may be test requirements by law which have to be complied with. If you have to do them, but are opposed to them in principle, you can take either what we call 'avoidance' or 'embracement' actions. Firstly reflect on your own practices to see how far you honour the principles you espouse.

Reflection This is a matter of conscience, but can you say that you *always:*

- Assign children to different groups according to the nature of the task, rather than according to their overall performance in school?
- Allow children to gradually extend their range of competence?
- Allow peer group teaching by getting children who have already mastered something to show others what to do?

The obverse of these practices is to:

- Label children as of this ability or that
- Let children concentrate on rehearsing their current level of performance
- Discourage group effort, discussion and talk, in favour of individual effort.

The majority of teachers follow the latter list for at least some of the time, and when you examine each statement you will find that they are all common basic ideas behind traditional tests. In other words no teacher is totally antipathetic to the principles behind testing.

Action *Avoidance:* Tie in your assessment with your teaching (this may be what you have always done). Assessment tied to teaching is not testing, providing that your judgements are *never* used for labelling. For example, you may not choose Clive to monitor your classroom experiments daily because he is unreliable or cannot record well enough. Before long Clive will know about your assessments and his subsequent labelling. It is your job to devise learning experiences which give Clive the chance to acquire the experience, knowledge, skills or whatever he needs, to avoid the label. Alternatively you might enable Clive to gain other expertise and take on other responsibilities so that the label regarding classroom experiments is not significant. Beware labelling him as the child who *can* do other things to the exclusion of Craig or Wilson or Ahmed!

Embracement: Offer to become the school consultant on assessment. With the help of the official documentation, the local advisory team and a librarian at a higher education establishment, devise a reading list. Really get to know about all the shortcomings of tests. You will then know exactly how to interpret test results. You will be able to advise colleagues on how to assess without labelling.

Try to develop your career path so that within a short time you have the chance to administer external tests. You will know how to handle what you have to do sensitively, and you will not be attracted by the possibilities of teaching to test.

Test capability

People sometimes do better in tests if they have done tests of the same kind before. If you are working with a class of children who have never done work in the kinds of ways which are expected for them to complete an external test, then it is fair to give them the opportunity to acquire the skills for carrying through tests. We must be clear that this is not *teaching to test;* experience of flexible ways of working has merit as learning in its own right, and can be put to good use outside school.

Reflection Which aspects of test situations have the children not met? Here are some examples:

- Assembling what they need for a task
- Completing a job with little teacher intervention
- Working in a group
- Doing something different from the rest of the class
- Suggesting ways of finding something out
- Predicting the outcomes of action
- Suggesting the next experiment on the basis of results they already have.

Action When you have a list of experiences which you feel the children lack, devise a timetable which will specifically permit them to try these. Start with one skill at a time and for a short time only. Gradually increase the complexity of your expectations and the length of time over which they should be carried out.

If, for example, you feel that the children in your present class are not very good at devising experiments, try these ideas:

- Play 'free thinking' games such as 'What could this be?' Hold up an orange for example. They may say it could be the sun, planet, space station, globe, eyeball, odd-shaped egg, fortune teller's ball, ball, a parcel of wheels, etc. Alternatively: 'What could you do with this?' Show a button or handkerchief. The aim is to get children thinking more broadly.

- Try getting them to invent as many ways as they can to wake a member of their family in the morning or fry an egg or get to school.
- Use National Curriculum Technology to get them to try and discard ideas and try again in looking for the best way of doing something.

Play free thinking games

Above all, be encouraging and accepting. There may be children in the class who are more creative than you are in the area of learning you are trying to explore, and it is important not to limit their thinking by comparing it with your own.

If group work is unfamiliar to the children, try setting up a problem-solving project or task

such as investigation of sounds around the school. Decide how you are to assign children to this workgroup. You may choose the composition of the group on the basis of the following:

- Past performance in science, for this work could contribute to science AT 12 Level 3
- Social maturity, for if you feel they can carry through the work collectively with confidence, then other children will see how group work is done
- Friendship, since an established social group can sometimes work well together
- Mixed ability, so that more able children can help the less able ones
- Specific skills, where, for example, one child is a popular leader, another has technical skills and another exceptional knowledge in science.

This all sounds rather complex. However, the grouping of children is important, for it can profoundly affect the quality of their learning, or indeed whether they learn at all. More advice about group work is given in Chapter 6.

Issue: Pressure from parents and friends

Parental pressure

This term may be used by some teachers as an excuse for preventing the implementation of change. We know teachers who say that they have to, for example, have weekly spelling tests, reading schemes and nothing messy in the classroom because of parental pressure. We know some headteachers who never elect to have a student teacher gain experience in their schools because of what they see as parental pressure. There are also some head-teachers who insist on year group classes whatever the current demographic composition of the school, because of that same pressure. We do not doubt that parental opinion can be felt by teachers, but opinions can be changed. Those teachers who cite outside pressure as a reason for doing or not doing things are avoiding their responsibility to address the problems, and that is thoroughly unprofessional.

How would you feel if your children's class-teacher said that your children were being taught in a certain way because of pressure from other children's parents? Surely you would expect to be able to trust the teacher to use his or her professional freedom to teach your children in the ways that were best for them. Now we have the prospect of teachers administering batteries of tests to children, and then saying that parental pressure for results 'at any price' forces them to do it. This is nonsense. Do not be persuaded that parental pressure on you, the teacher, and thereby the children, cannot be turned to good effect.

If you believe the children *really* are under parental pressure, you must first assure yourself that this is so through first-hand contact with parents. Then you should, in the interests of the children, try to find out why that pressure is applied.

Reflection   What is the best way to approach the parents? If it is Miranda who is most anxious about always getting a tick, and who cries rather than asks for help, it is Miranda and her parents whom you should talk to. If there is a general anxiety in the class, and you feel that many parents may be concerned, reflect on what it is you wish to say to reassure them. You may wish to say things like:

● The children are not in a race, but at the beginning of a process called education which will last all their lives
● Anxious children do not seem to learn as well or be as confident as relaxed ones

● What children write in their books does not reflect all they learn, and it may be that on days when they say they have done 'nothing', they learned most
● Repeated testing of children does nothing to improve the quality of their education
● Teachers are there to help children work at their optimum; that is to do their best without undue stress, and that is your intention.

Action   About a single child like Miranda, let the headteacher know of your concerns, and invite Miranda and her parents to come and talk to you after school. With Miranda and her parents, share your concern that each child should do their best, show them her progress, and comment on work well done. Mention the areas in which Miranda and you need to invest more time. Assure her parents that she is working hard and that what you expect is her optimum learning without undue stress. Carry through a promise to let them know regularly how Miranda is doing in school.

If the pressure from parents seems to be on many children, discuss the issue and what

Invite the parents to come into school

21

you propose to say with your headteacher, and invite the parents to an evening meeting where you can broadcast your ideas.

To an audience of parents you need to express your own convictions about all children working at their optimum, and the dangers of forcing children to work under stress. Invite their collaboration in three ways, by asking them to:

- Avoid making their children worry about their schoolwork
- Help their children in developing special interests outside school
- Help their children's classteacher in resourcing topic work.

Peer group pressure

There is a rather sentimental poster issued by the Scottish Health Education Group entitled 'Children Learn what they Live'. The underlying message is for compassion, and among the things children should live with, it lists encouragement, praise, approval, acceptance and friendship. In primary classrooms there can develop an ethos which includes all these things, and it is up to the teacher to embody that ethos. If assessment is not allowed to sully our humanitarianism, then teachers can help children to view one another as whole human beings, and not as 'brainy', 'dumbo', 'hopeless' or 'swot'. Working lives of future adults may well centre more on talents which have not been given high status in the education system; these include flexibility, co-operation, creativity and oral skills. These skills may transcend examinable skills, and children need to be helped to view themselves as developing whole people, not ciphers at the bottom of an achievement ladder.

Reflection If there does seem to be a prevailing myth about the importance of 'cleverness' or lack of it in your class, it may be a good idea to reflect on how that has come about. These questions may help:

- What are the home backgrounds of the children like, and is peer group pressure an issue to tackle with parents?
- Who are the most popular children?
- Who are those who excel academically and are they popular?
- Does the composition of the class, or groups within it, support the myth?
- Is the prevailing view associated with other unwelcome prejudice such as male chauvinism or racism?

Action Praise, praise, praise, for human virtues such as helpfulness, gentleness and perseverance rather than for academic achievement. The influential and outspoken children in the class are the particular individuals who can support and implement change. You may also like to consider carrying through some of these ideas with the class:

- A debate about the 'best people we know' and what we like about them
- A speaker to talk about teamwork and helping others
- A questionnaire about men and women of compassion in history and great people in the world today
- A whole-school project about caring.

At some point in the development of the new ethos you can start to introduce group work with groups composed in unorthodox ways. The challenge is to set problems that can be worked on by the whole group in ways that give everyone the chance to make a contribution. The outcome of the work needs to be a 'presentation' where everyone feels proud of the collective effort, and begins to realise the benefits in collaborative work with people possessing a variety of strengths.

A sample presentation

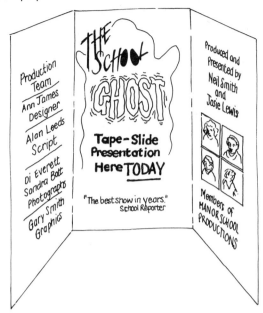

Issue: Teaching time and assessment time and coverage

Time for assessment: continuous and terminal

It is regrettable that, while time for reflection on pupil progress and for evaluation is just as important for the reception class teacher as for the teacher in higher education, the former is provided with no such time at all during the course of his or her work. It is teachers in primary schools who are most concerned about lack of time for assessment because they already have full timetables, little or no non-contact time and constant personal demands made on them.

When we look at timing and assessment we need to distinguish between continuous (teacher assessments) and terminal (external) judgements, although both kinds of assessment can carry similar management problems. There is no more time to devote to assessment,

so how can it be done? The official reply is to assess in the course of your work. Gathering impressions has always been part of teachers' work, and they have done it all the time. More systematic observation and data collection is only possible through highly expert management of all the factors affecting assessment. (There is more discussion of these management issues in Chapter 6.) It does have to be done, and in ways that produce information that makes sense to other people. Let us look firstly at continuous assessment.

Reflection   You do need to reflect on exactly why it is that you feel timing and continuous assessment are a problem for you. It may be that one of the following factors contributes to your problems:

- Your classroom layout does not make the observation of children easy
- Children are not working in ways that enable you to listen to and observe group work
- Written work has not been sampled effectively to do detailed assessments
- There have been limited opportunities to liaise with colleagues about teaching and assessment management.

Action   Change! Establish what is the most important thing to change, then do so. In your own classroom try one thing at a time, taking the most important first. You may, for example, make the layout of the room more open, get the children to work more independently of you, and sample written work on a manageable basis, for assessment purposes (for example, one in 10 or 15 pieces).

To enhance the possibilities of liaison with colleagues ask the headteacher if there can be whole staff or whole department meetings to discuss time and assessment. The outcomes of these meetings will depend on the flexibility of the staff and their needs. Ad hoc arrangements to have two classes for TV or story-time are not an answer, and must be resisted. What you really need are regular blocks of time when you can be with perhaps one child, or even half the class, but not all of them. One solution may be more co-operative teaching.

If we look at terminal assessment of children, including multi-task tests like SATs, some of the problems such as opportunities for listening, observation and liaison with colleagues are the same as for continuous assessment. Formal tests do present additional problems, since their prescribed timing schedule, if there is one, must be followed.

Reflection   In administering any formal test, there are test-specific rules about how to give it. If the rules are not followed, then the test is rendered invalid. (There is more discussion of this in Chapter 4.) You therefore need to check the rules of administration for any external test you are asked to give the children, and reflect on what this means for the time management of your classroom.

Action   Ask your colleagues and head-teacher to help you ensure that required test conditions are met.

Assessment by sampling

It would be patently ridiculous to expect teachers to assess every child on every statement of attainment in every foundation subject under test conditions. The present intention to sample for external tests is more realistic in the context of a working classroom. For these assessments much of the sampled content is predetermined. This places an appropriate emphasis on teachers' judgements of all the other things the children are learning. You will, therefore, have to sample children for specific observation and pieces of written work for specific scrutiny. You do not have to meet rigorous conditions to do this. It avoids all of the problems that beset 'scientific'

judgements, except one: bias. We talk about this issue in Chapter 3.

There are two causes for concern here. We should avoid giving undue weight to those performances sampled for external tests, and try to avoid a cumulative levelling-down in our overall judgement of children. There is also a genuinely felt pressure: teachers feel compelled to mark all of the children's written work! This is commonly done to meet parental demands and expectations. To this is often added the concern that the headteacher makes judgements about the effort of individual teachers partly on the basis of their regular and thorough marking.

Reflection   The issue is not whether to sample, but how to do it. The answers will be personal ones dependent on you and your favoured ways of working.

Action   Predetermine a period of time, perhaps four weeks, where you intend to sample children's written work, perhaps in English. Discuss this with the headteacher and use this discussion to help refine a list of the aspects of written English which you are intending to analyse critically. Work out a sampling system that permits you to sample at least two pieces of written work for each child. In marking these pieces look for the new learning needs for each child, using your list of items as an *aide-mémoire*. With the help of the headteacher and other colleagues evaluate the outcomes of your experiment. In undertaking this evaluation it is essential that the emphasis is put on the quality of the information you have gathered, not its quantity.

As a result of your reflection you may decide to focus your assessments for short periods of time on the following:

● A group of children within the class who may be defined by one of a number of factors, for example, English is their second

The child is the focus in this record

MATHEMATICS CHILD RECORD: level 1 NAME: _Leyla Hill_ CLASS(ES): **1**		INTRODUCED	WORKED ON	MASTERED	TEACHER'S COMMENTS
PC1 AT: 1	(Number/measures) Use materials Talk/ask questions Predict				
2	Numbers to 10 Conserve	/ Sound work to 5 /	< using numbers to 10 < to 5	△ Good understanding	Grasped number quickly
3	+ − to 10	/ add / take to 5/7/10	< much practical	△ concept needs experience of presentation	Try vertical Present.
4	Estimate to 10				
5	Repeat patterns				
8	Compare/order objects (pre-measure)				

This supplies the teacher with a detailed record of contact with an area of the curriculum for a group or class

MATHEMATICS AT3 level 1 (I = I contact / = mastered)							TEACHER'S RECORD SHEET
Name of child	Addition without recording to 10	Addition with some recording to 10	Subtraction without recording to 10	Subtraction with some recording to 10	Formal addition to 10	Formal subtraction to 10	Teacher's comments
Leyla Hill	IIIIIIIIII ⁄	IIIIIIIIIII IIII ⁄	IIIII ⁄	IIIIIIIIII ⁄	IIII	IIII	needs unorthodox presentations.
Roberta Linby	IIIIIIIIIIIIIII ⁄	IIIIIIIII ⁄	II				

Reproduced from Clemson D. and Clemson W., *The Really Practical Guide to National Curriculum 5-11* (1989)

language, or they commonly work together
● A sector of the curriculum.

Both approaches require a variety of methods, of which there is more discussion in Chapter 4.

The recording devices you use will be either those attached to each child, or subject records (see above).

We all recognise that to some extent this is a

spurious way to divide the work children have done. Records and assessments always register the dynamic interplay between a child and a task. So long as we bear this in mind, we can be pragmatic about choosing 'children' or 'task' as the category about which we make recordings. A rule of thumb for which to select lies in what it is going to be used for. There are examples of suggested layouts for records in Chapter 5.

Depending on the kind of record you are making you can then determine the feasible level of sampling: it may be the observation of the sample group of children for 15 minutes three times a week, or it may include looking at one in 10 of the pieces of work a child does. It is likely that you will only be able to systematise your assessments with careful planning. Setting up the plans is arduous, but once in place they do help you to get the information you need. They do not rule out serendipity either. When Douglas suddenly leaps up and says, 'I've got it, yes, I see,' you can use that information too.

Issue: What is being assessed

Defining what to assess

The official documentation and other publications about National Curriculum assessment seem to use an individual statement of attainment as a 'unit of knowledge' around which assessment of children should be arranged.

There are many problems in carrying through this idea. The important ones are the following:

- The statements of attainment are a 'mixed bag' and therefore require sophisticated matching with appropriate ways of testing
- There are far too many such statements for

it to be possible to assess each one for every child
- Some statements of attainment represent large 'parcels' of learning while others represent little learning; they may therefore need varying amounts of assessment
- Some statements of attainment are subject bound while others are not
- Some statements of attainment are locked between the one preceding and the one following and have to be taught and assessed in sequence, while others do not.

However, the statements of attainment are still the best place to start, for they represent, to the world outside your classroom, what it is that children should learn. You may also wish to assess children's capacities beyond the confines of the National Curriculum or in areas unrelated to academic achievement. Whether they are part of the National Curriculum or not, you should be able to reflect on the sorts of things you are assessing.

Reflection Analyse the statements of attainment, or the aspects of children's performance that you are assessing. Try to work out, for example, whether you are interested in:

- How Carolyn approaches and sets up the task
- How she actually carries out the practical work
- What instruments Carolyn uses in her experiments and whether she demonstrates that she can take accurate readings
- How she sets down what she does and her results
- How Carolyn feels about science, or practical work, or working alone.

For a fuller discussion of what to assess and how, refer to Chapter 4.

Action Create a mental or an actual flowchart which has at least these elements:

- Relevant statements of attainment, or details of attitudes, etc.
- What the children actually do
- The bits of what they do which will enable you to make an assessment
- How you are going to collect that information
- What the possible judgements are
- Pointers for the future.

Performance on test

We all know that we behave differently in different settings. Some of us may be first-class cooks who seem to always make a mess of things when we have guests. Good public speakers may find that they perform best with an audience of strangers and are tongue-tied at a family gathering. Some sports teams play better on their home ground, while others do better away. Some people make great strides doing the same kind of thing in the same setting again and again; others stop making any progress after two similar tries and need to approach a task differently each time.

There are two important points for teachers contained in these examples. The first is that children only show some of their 'performances' at school, and these may not be their best ones. This has important implications for the idea of a 'whole child' approach and for things parents and others may say about individual children in your care. The second point is that real assessment of the children in relation to task is only truly possible by matching each child to an appropriate assessment situation.

You may say that to be a good cook you have to cook well, no matter who it is for; this is to take an external exam-oriented and 'end-point' approach to cooking. In continuous, formative assessment of young children, we must limit the effects of external factors such as situation, audience and so on, and make the assessment reflect, as far as we possibly can,

An example of an assessment flowchart

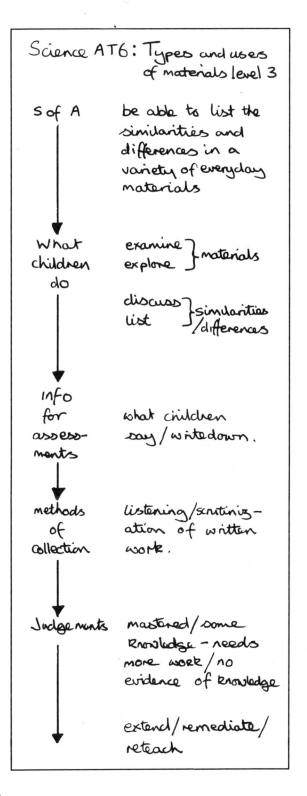

Science AT6: Types and uses of materials level 3

S of A — be able to list the similarities and differences in a variety of everyday materials

What children do — examine / explore } materials

discuss / list } similarities / differences

Info for assessments — what children say / write down.

methods of collection — listening / scrutinisation of written work.

Judgements — mastered / some knowledge - needs more work / no evidence of knowledge

extend / remediate / reteach

27

on just child and task. That is the challenge. Many of us have had a child in our class from time to time, of whom we may have said, 'I have this feeling Jamie can do it, but I can't get him to show me that he can!' The teacher as assessor has to set up the task so that Jamie can show he *can* do it! Once Jamie has succeeded in one particular set of circumstances that have been carefully devised by the teacher, then he or she can help him to generalise his success. The intention is that eventually he should be like the 'good cook': a good cook in his own view, a good cook in the eyes of other people, and a cook for whom an external demonstration of skill (for example an exam) is no problem.

Mercifully, teacher assessment means you rarely have to sample just one performance to make an assessment. Children can show you some of their better performances, and you can ignore their 'off' days.

Performances in tests that are externally devised, on the other hand, though they may be worked over a period of time, are almost one-off performances. The results of these are important because they are currently being given more credibility than other assessments by people outside school. Your responsibility is to see that the children are given the best possible chance to demonstrate their present capabilities under these conditions. If they underperform, you will still feel you did your best, and you should have the opportunity to declare the mismatch between your expectations and the actual performance.

Reflection   For example, Gareth has demonstrated performances at level 3 in science consistently in his top infant year. A project called 'Growing' was started in the summer term and a test incorporating scientific enquiry was done in the course of this work. Over the three-week period, when the teacher was compiling her assessments, Gareth's work showed uncharacteristic sloppiness and brevity.

Action   No teacher with experience in primary schools would see the justice in assigning Gareth a 'level 2' tick on a record sheet as a measure of his performance level at the end of key stage 1. For teachers in primary schools the class performance must be matched against the performance on test. If there is a mismatch, it does mean that you must check Gareth's past work and make sure that nothing went awry. For example:

- Did his oral skills mask lack of basic understanding?
- Was he relying too heavily on the contribution of other children?
- Was he copying other children's work?

If Gareth's work does not indicate any of these problems, then you should have the chance to assign him to level 3 and substantiate your grading with work samples for moderators to see.

Issue: Recording assessments

Tidiness

There is a short answer to this one. You *must* keep tidy detailed records! You may have considered the attribute of tidiness to be common in people who are slightly obsessional but unimaginative. You may not see tidiness as a characteristic you wish to acquire, for you may feel you may thereby lose your individually creative image. You will, however, have to cultivate the former without compromising the latter! It is part of your job as a manager of teaching and learning to communicate your judgements. If you are really not prepared to arrange what you write as an intelligible form of communication, both for yourself and other people, you risk wasting your own time and that of colleagues and the children.

ENGLISH AT1 L1 CHILD RECORD	NAME O. Harris	ASSESSMENT PERIOD: March 1 - 14 1990
Date	1/3	5/3
Speak / listen in group / play	Shy in whole class news time. More forthcoming in playhouse - took lead in assigning roles	Spoke up in work group discussion (science AT 3 L1)
Date	2/3	
listen well / respond	Finds it difficult to sit still unless there is a picture to look at while story read. Does not offer contributions	
Date	2/3	5/3
follow instructions	Follows one simple instruction	Keen interest in science - follows instructions about resourcing and activity.

A tidy record: legible and intelligible to yourself and colleagues

Reflection

What is it that is a problem for you? It may be one of the following:

- Your handwriting
- Lack of appropriate stationery
- Lack of organisation
- Lack of space in the classroom
- Lack of technical skill in setting things out.

Action

Remediate your poor handwriting and lack of layout skills by doing a course. As a short-term measure, if you have a colleague with a parallel or similar class, ask if you may collaborate on the choice of stationery, setting out forms, and organising writing space, etc. Do not let him or her do it for you, but make it clear that these are things that you, yourself, need to improve.

Form-filling

Teachers are often wary of branding children for life by making an extremely favourable or critical remark on an official form. It is a job to be taken seriously, and often records do follow children throughout their school career. However, there is little point in completing a form unless it reflects your true judgements of how a child has progressed while in your care.

The kinds of assessments teachers have always made for themselves have been recorded in idiosyncratic ways. Hand-on forms have been the most standard. It is common for schools to use standard internal record forms which may date from a long while ago, or have forms which are consistent across a local education authority or which have been compiled within the school. It does not matter what the layout of the form is like *so long as it does not preclude you from declaring what you consider vital.* Whatever you do, do not leave out anything crucial just because a form did not ask for it or did not allow space for the comments or information. The form should also be intelligible to everyone allowed access to it, and there should be a level of common understanding about what it means.

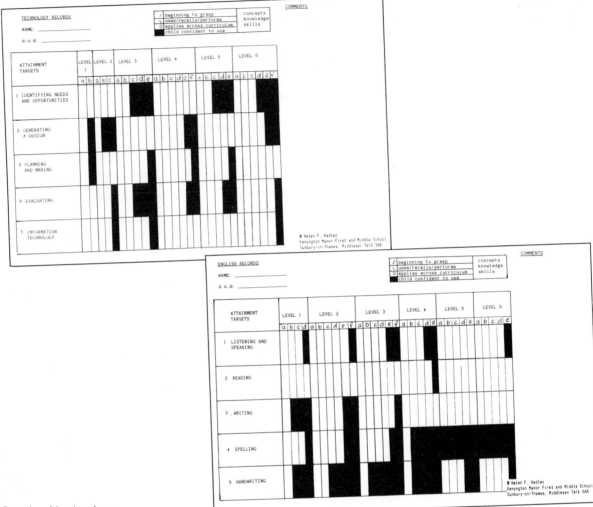

Examples of hand-on forms

It seems likely that forms will require some modification or redesigning to allow entries related to achievement in National Curriculum foundation subjects. The development of profiling is also discussed in Chapter 5. Such forms will be new in many primary schools. Dilemmas associated with designing new forms are also dealt with in Chapter 5.

Before you reflect on how a form you have to complete should be changed to fit your predilections, find out:

● Who devised it
● Who else has to complete forms like it
● The audience for whom it is intended.

Reflection The more local the form and the smaller its audience, the easier it may be to ask for modifications. Once you know these facts, you will be able to reflect, realistically, on what change you can hope for and who to approach.

Action If the form is internal to the school, talk to the assessment co-ordinator or head-teacher about your concerns. Be prepared to put forward written suggestions and even a mock-up of a redesigned form. If appropriate, suggested layouts could be shared at a staff meeting, in order that a common under-standing about the form can be reached. Do remember though, that every new member of staff will then need to acquire this understanding too.

If the form is one approved by the local authority, you will need the support of your colleagues and headteacher to instigate change.

Issue: Teacher as expert assessor

We are sometimes able to make better judgements when we have more information and have met similar situations before. This applies to the judgements we make about children's progress. However, increased experience may make us confident of our verdicts to the point of inflexibility. Because every human being is different, it is important to take note of each child's uniqueness, and not just say, for example, 'She's just like Rachel I taught five years ago', or 'His work reminds me so much of Suchit's'.

Reflection Think about what aspects of assessment you are underconfident about and get help with those. It may be useful to look at later chapters of this book in order to identify whether it is techniques or management issues which feature uppermost in your list of difficulties. Remember that the chief emphasis of the teacher as assessor is to make judgements about a child in relation to a task (criterion-referenced assessment). It therefore does not matter whether this is your first class or your thirtieth; you do not need to compare one child with another, so you do not need to have taught dozens of children to make sound assessment judgements.

Action If you lack confidence with techniques, read about them and experiment with them. If management problems need to be sorted out, then you may need the help of a colleague in establishing what it is that you change first. Becoming an expert depends on application, knowledge and practice; even

with these three things, if you still find that making judgements about progress is a problem, then ask for 'a second opinion' about some of the children in your class who are known to other teachers. Sharing insights will help you learn how other teachers carry out assessment, and identify refinements you can make to your own ways of making judgements.

Summary

This chapter has presented some of the obstacles to doing assessment. If any of these match your own feelings, we hope that you have been able to use the sections on reflection and action to good effect and that you will find the problem resolvable.

The underlying message of this chapter is that many of the obstacles to assessment are actually within ourselves and our perceptions about possible ways of working. We are all products of our experience and may therefore, to some extent, be bound by our own personal and professional histories. However, education is actually about change, and that includes teachers as well as learners. We cannot exclude ourselves from that process of change!

There *are* real constraints to do with time and resources. More investment in education *is* vital in order to give teachers more time for analysis and reflection and so that they can help children to realise their potential. But we also believe that there are some significant things that we can all do within the existing constraints. Our comments, though contentious, may provoke a rethinking of your own views and constructive dialogue in school. The remaining chapters of the book are intended to help you increase your expertise now that you have, we hope, started to overcome your concerns about the whole business of assessment.

3

MASTERING JARGON, TOOLS AND RULES

Like any regulated human activity, assessment has its own set of procedures, rules and technical terms. The rules have been built up over many years. They embrace the concepts of fairness, appropriateness and merit. Cheating is not allowed. However, some of the rules and terms in assessment are complex and open to honest misinterpretation or inappropriate application. It is important, therefore, that everyone in education should get to grips with the language of assessment and the principles behind assessment methods and outcomes, so that we do not misuse them or make mistakes.

In learning the ground rules for assessment there are three major areas we need to address:

● The broad distinctions between types of assessment
● Possible uses for assessments
● The role of assessor and the interpretation of assessment data.

In each of these areas there are qualitative and quantitative features which need to be understood. The qualitative aspects include being able to use assessment tools and interpret outcomes, and the quantitative aspects include some underlying statistical principles. Andrew Lange (1844–1912) is reported to have said, *'He uses statistics as a drunken man uses lamp-posts – for support rather than illumination'* (Treasury of Humorous Quotations). In the field of assessment, it is illumination rather than support that we are after! It is important to be able to select an assessment approach on the basis of an understanding of the nature of that approach, its validity, its possible outcomes and its impact on children's learning. Whilst this chapter will be neither exhaustive nor exhausting, it is intended to let you know enough to become a confident assessor.

Kinds of assessment

Distinguishing types of assessment

In undertaking assessments of children it is important to be clear whether we are measuring their work against predetermined criteria or whether we are trying to place them in relation to other children and their work. This demands reflection and analysis, for the same assessment tool can often be used in either of these ways.

The expectations behind the assessment of children in relation to National Curriculum work are not clear cut. On the one hand teachers are going to have to assess individual children against the criteria made explicit in statements of attainment; on the other hand teachers will have to put their 'results' alongside those of groups of children across the nation. This means that there are official requirements to use teacher assessments as both criterion- and norm-referenced tools. It is therefore essential that we see clearly the emphases in both kinds of referencing so that we can use them appropriately.

Criterion-referenced assessment   This is one of the two main approaches we adopt in assessing the children in our care. For some tasks we measure the achievement against the task itself. In other words we identify the characteristics and requirements for the successful achievement of a task and deem that individual children have achieved the task when those characteristics are shown or the requirements have been met or exceeded.

For example:

Teacher to Sally: 'Go and choose a poem from one of the poetry books and copy it into your exercise book.'

There is no suggestion, in the way the task is set, that Sally's work will be compared with that of other children. If Sally succeeds in complying with the teacher's instruction, she will have met the teacher's assessment criteria. This is a criterion-referenced situation. The teacher would not have asked Sally to do all this if there was not a reasonable chance that Sally could do it. This is an important aspect of criterion-referenced assessments: that is, you do not attempt the 'test' until you have a good chance of success.

This sort of assessment is commonly found in the context of motor skills such as the correct hold and skilful use of scissors or a tennis racket, but the use of this approach will become more common in all areas of the curriculum.

Examples of activities which are readily criterion-referenced are:

● Hopping
● Swimming a length of the pool

● Knowing your address or telephone number
● Tying shoelaces
● Putting a story in sequence order
● Measuring a given quantity to a given degree of accuracy
● Mastering number bonds up to 10.

Engage the children in criterion-referenced activities

Norm-referenced assessment   The other main approach to assessment is concerned with locating children's work in relation not only to the task, but also to the work of others. In other words we are rating, and therefore ranking, the child on a scale which ranges typically from excellent to poor. Examples of this sort of assessment are common and include marks out of 10 or 100, grades A–E, positions 1st–35th and so on. These are norm-referenced assessments.

For example:

Teacher to class: 'Copy the weather chart and the key to the symbols into your project folder.'

In this case John, for example, has to carry out a task which can be compared directly with the performance of other children on exactly the same task. John's work can be set against a range of norms related to handwriting skill, layout and presentation that the teacher will have in mind. This is a norm-referenced situation.

Other examples of norm-referencing are:

- Reading a graded book in a reading scheme
- Coming third in a race
- Winning a prize for good behaviour
- Speaking more clearly and articulately than some other children
- Getting 9 out of 10 in creative writing.

You can see from the examples that there are some crucial differences between criterion- and norm-referenced assessments. These are shown in Figure 3.1.

Figure 3.1 A comparison of criterion and norm-referenced assessments

CRITERION-REFERENCED	NORM-REFERENCED
Careful and unambiguous construction of criteria related to task (can/cannot do)	Constructed with comparison possibilities between individuals (spread of performance possible)
Clearly observable information, little interpretative judgement	Not always observable information, much interpretative judgement
Always use criteria external to the individuals tested	Sometimes involve criteria related to individuals tested

The final point on this chart comparing criterion-referenced and norm-referenced assessments needs clarification. You may, for example, test the ball skills of children in the class, and set a 'test' requiring them to catch eight out of ten balls thrown from a specified distance. Perhaps only some children will be able to do it. The possibility that a child will be able to achieve a 'tick' for ball skills is unaffected by the achievement of other children in the same class or other classes, or indeed children in other schools. By contrast, norm-referencing can occur within the narrow confines of a particular group. For example, it is possible to have someone near the bottom of the class in reading who might be top in other classes! In theory it should be impossible to have this sort of discrimination in a criterion-referenced situation. Take the case of a driving test: it does not matter where you take the test: if you meet the criteria for passing, you will pass.

How assessments are used

Whether assessments are norm- or criterion-referenced they can be used for different purposes. Assessment outcomes can be used in the following ways:

- For reporting purposes at the end of a particular phase or experience (summative)
- To indicate stages reached and then to help identify areas for subsequent work and development (formative)
- To identify particular learning difficulties for an individual child (diagnostic)
- To reflect on the teaching and the learning (evaluative).

A single assessment is rarely put to all these uses, but we would expect to find assessments used in all these ways in a primary classroom over a period of time. Many of them may be informal, often intuitive and frequently recurring. Assessment is not just 'the big test'.

Summative and formative assessment

The 'achievement equals end-point' view, which is often called 'summative', is a powerful one. It means considering assessment as being about what *has been* achieved rather than indicating what *might be* achieved. A contrasting view of assessment is that it should be used to illuminate the next steps, so that the learners regard it as having future purpose. This is known as 'formative' assessment.

Not everyone is convinced of the role of assessment as a formative influence on learning, as the law and the views of 'the man in the street' would testify. However, whilst learning and new teaching are not inextricably linked in the legal requirements, there is support for the suggestion that assessment can be continuous and formative. The Task Group on Assessment and Testing which was set up by the Government to make recommendations in these areas say in their report,

> **"***Promoting children's learning is a principal aim of schools. Assessment lies at the heart of this process.***"**
> A Report. National Curriculum Task Group on Assessment and Testing. (DES and the Welsh Office. 1987)

The work of the SEAC seems to endorse this view. They say:

> **"***A single assessment process is able to inform teachers' decisions about how to tackle children's learning needs.***"**
> A Guide to Teacher Assessment. Pack C. A Source Book of Teacher Assessment (SEAC, 1990) l. 4, p. 4

Summative assessment: examinations Formal examinations are clearly summative experiences. They coincide with perceived end-points within the system. Their purpose is to identify individual achievement against a predetermined body of knowledge. Examinations are characterised by being content-centred and by offering minimal feedback. We obtain a grade or percentage but no indication of ways to improve our future performance or even to identify particular areas of weakness. Examinations tend to offer global judgements which are reduced to single outcome statements. Examinations offered to large numbers of candidates are not constructed (nor could they be) for the individual; rather they offer 'norms' against which individuals test themselves.

Formative assessment: continuous Assessments which take place at regular intervals and offer opportunities for detailed feedback are 'continuous'. Such assessments are characterised by concern not only for content but also for individual development. Learners expect to receive feedback on areas of strength and weakness and to be given guidance on how to improve their future performance.

Assessment in the primary school is on the whole formative and continuous. It is still the case that in primary schooling summative assessments are made exclusively as a result of external demands. The teacher of children of primary school age is always looking forward, and this is a formative perspective. It is this vision of the child's future in learning that guides teaching and grants the child opportunities.

Other uses

Diagnostic assessment When a teacher finds that a particular child is having problems with an area of learning, he or she tries to find out why. He or she may remediate by re-teaching using a different method, and then if problems persist, he or she will work individually with the child to try to discover where the conceptual difficulties are. In primary schools reading is a major area of work in which diagnostic tests are used. With the advent of the National Curriculum it is clear that there is a need to become expert in diagnosis in areas of the curriculum other than reading.

Here is an example from a top infant class working on a mathematical topic involving the use of number bonds. The children were rolling two dice and using the numbers on each one to make up some 'sums' and statements about numbers. One little girl, Rebecca, threw a one and a three. She said:

> **"**If you put those numbers side by side it could be 13 or 31
> If you times them together you get three
> If you add them you get four
> If you take the one away from the three you get two
> If you take the three away from the one you get nothing.**"**

From what Rebecca said, it seems that she has no concept of whole negative numbers. Further work would need to be done to establish that this was the case, but here there is a clear opening for diagnostic assessment.

Indeed, as the requirement for being familiar with whole negative numbers occurs in Mathematics Level 3, AT 2 on Number, this may be about the right time for Rebecca to be engaging in this sort of work. This example also shows that assessments have a diagnostic use for children performing within the average range, as well as those working above or below it.

The common use of the words 'diagnostic tests' by educational psychologists and others, when attempting to help children with marked difficulties, may have led some teachers to see 'diagnosis' as having no part in their normal classroom role. On the contrary, diagnosis is what teachers do intuitively. How much more powerful your impressions about individuals become if you systematise them and refer to them as diagnostic assessments!

Examples of diagnostic tests

Why are you been late?

1. Granny bought she me an ice-cream.
2. Janet often reads a story chair.
3. An elephant eats has a large trunk.
4. I like to watching television.
5. The cat plays is asleep.
6. I am going for home now.
7. Whose is this book kittens?
8. Boys like playing football with.
9. How far is your mother?
10. Who is your house in this street?

feet	big	children	(tall)	have.
1. hungry	children	always	are.	
2. chocolate	likes	Peter	eating.	
3. television	often	watch	I.	
4. me my	teacher	than	bigger	is.
5. how	to	teach	swim	me.
6. play	like	would	who	to?
7. school	going	teacher	is	to.
8. school	tired	of	are	we.
9. start	when	I'll	to	you	tell.

Evaluative assessment All the work done by a class can be used to provide evaluative assessments. These may, for example, be used to determine the efficacy of prior teaching, the merits of doing a particular piece of work, when and how it was done and the usefulness to a child of being in a particular work group.

In making evaluative assessments it is important to take note of the interplay between yourself (the teacher), the child and the task. These can be linked diagrammatically as shown in Figure 3.2.

Figure 3.2 Starting points for evaluative assessment

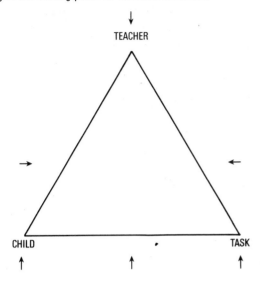

You can take as a starting point for the evaluation any of the following:

- Teacher
- Teacher – Task
- Teacher – Child
- Child
- Child – Task
- Task

Ways of using these as starting points for evaluation are spelled out in Clemson, D. and Clemson, W. *The Really Practical Guide to National Curriculum 5–11* (1989). In this book we will give an example that relates specifically to the child-task link, which we see as the area for formative assessment. Note that all the

An evaluation example

Teaching activities Counting to 100, counting in 10s, 'play' with 1p and 10p coins, Cuisenaire and Colour factor 10s and 1s, play as a cashier where customers need 10p coins to 'have a go' on games around the room and can swap their 1p coins, number squares to 100, writing numbers 0-100 and an investigation of where we put the digits, oral maths: e.g. how many tens in 35, what do four tens and two make and how do we write it, what do we say this is : 92? and this 29? How are they different? Would you rather have 15p or 51p pocket-money and why?

Group taught: The Skylarks - Ben, Derek, Ruth, Davina, Liz and Matthew, all working on ATs 2 and 4, Level 3.

Outcomes On the basis of assessment of practical activities by observation and all written work produced on the concept of number, it is apparent that the children have mastered place value except Derek, Liz and Matthew who need more consolidation work on place value.

Reflection and evaluation The tasks were a mismatch for the children who did not succeed. Though they know about equivalence they are confused about how to record numbers. They now need a special programme of activities to develop their confidence about numbers and how they are composed.

details of the evaluation are worked out. We realise that you may not need to record all these steps, but they do all need to be done, even if they are not written down, so that you can make evaluative judgements.

Being fair

Subjectivity and objectivity

To make a move from general impressions to detailed specific questions which are intended to inform 'objectively' is a giant step, but it is one that is familiar to teachers. Notions of objectivity can bedevil educational assessment. The word 'objective' is used widely by people working in the natural sciences. It is used to reinforce the requirement to control variables and replicate results in order to arrive at scientific 'truths'; but 'truth' in the assessment of human beings is much more problematic. Variables are difficult (if not impossible) to control, and we cannot really repeat an experiment. People who have already been involved in research are changed by it and so experiments cannot be done in exactly the same way with them again; a new sample of people is different, so the experiment is strictly speaking not the same as before. In fact, if we accept the notion that education is all about change, then a wholly scientific approach is entirely unsuitable.

When we, as teachers, are exhorted to be objective in our assessment of children we are really being asked to be unbiased and non-prejudicial in our judgements. This does not mean that we have to be scientific nor does it mean that we can, or should, rely exclusively on judgements made according to results of external tests. When making assessments about children's performance and potential we need to take account of these ideas concerning our decisions:

- None of our judgements are truly 'objective'
- Subjective assessment is valuable in education, even if it is undervalued
- Our judgements do need to be more than intuitive to be of value to others as well as ourselves
- Whilst recognising that our judgements will mix subjective and objective elements we do need to avoid bias.

Valid assessments depend, in our view, on teachers' own professional experience helping them to make unbiased judgements.

Validity and reliability

These concepts are extremely important in assessment, and they are linked ideas. *Validity* means that an assessment must assess what it is supposed to. This may sound obvious but, as we will see, numbers of assessments carried out in schools do not actually meet the essential criterion of validity! *Reliability* means that an assessment should be consistent. It is the degree to which, if the same children were given the same test on different occasions the pattern of results would be the same. In other words if you were to test children in, say, an element of mathematics, the test used should produce very similar results over a period of time and there should not be wildly differing results for individual children. It is possible, however, to have an assessment procedure or approach which meets the criterion of reliability but that is not valid. You can consistently hit the target, but it may be the wrong target! On the other hand high validity in an assessment task usually carries with it a high degree of reliability. You can only have real confidence in your judgements about assessment outcomes if the validity and reliability of the assessment approach is known. Some examples of situations will help to clarify these concepts, and also serve to illustrate how elusive they can be at times.

Many teachers give spelling tests. There are two main approaches. Children are given either:

(a) spellings of their own words or words associated with, say, a reading scheme which they are working through, or

(b) spellings of words deemed common or necessary by the teachers.

In situation (a) it should be possible to produce a valid set of words, as they will come directly from the children's experience. The way in which the tests (a) are given can, however, affect reliability. If teachers adopt different strategies with their classes, using different levels of formality, help and so on, then results within that class may vary greatly over time. This will, of course, undermine the whole validity of the enterprise across the school. In the case of (b) it is not possible, at the outset, to assume the validity of the chosen list of words. The words may only be met in the spelling test and not be used by the children in other contexts. The test becomes a test of memory rather than of spelling capability. Finally, in both cases (a) and (b), more investigation would need to be done to establish whether or not the assessment outcomes indicated transfer. Children might do well on the test but still not spell correctly in their own writing. It is therefore vital that we are certain that our spelling test is actually related to the development of spelling and not merely an exercise which fulfils its own needs, but no others.

This example of spelling tests applies in all areas where we are using an assigned task for the purposes of assessment. Statisticians offer us a range of ways to measure reliability, but these are beyond the scope of this book. Validity, though, is a concept that can be usefully explored further here. There are, in fact, five sorts of validity we need to consider; face, content, concurrent, predictive and construct validity. Many of these have been raised within the spelling discussion above – do not be put off by the jargon!

Face validity   This is often used in schools for making judgements about a range of things including, for example, the selection of mathematics schemes, plans for the school day and the selection of reading tests. The basic tenet here is that the materials, test or other resource to be used looks as though it meets the appropriate needs. There is nothing wrong in examining things for their face validity, but it is only a first and very preliminary step. It should be used to exclude; inclusion needs more analysis.

Content validity   This is of central importance to the teacher. The content of an assessment must match the content of the learning opportunities that the children have had. It is of no use to assess children against unfamiliar material. This is of central importance in looking at ways of assessing children in respect of the National Curriculum. There are, however, the concomitant dangers of 'teaching to test'. The content validity should arise from the teaching and learning and not from the test.

Concurrent validity   This refers to the degree to which the outcomes of an assessment are borne out in related and similar tasks or assessments. If we say that Elizabeth is at level 4 in the science assessment we have conducted, do we have evidence that Elizabeth is operating at level 4 in science in areas we did not assess at that time? Again this is of central concern in relation to the reporting of National Curriculum assessments.

Predictive validity   The question raised here is to what extent does the result of an assessment carry a prediction for the future? If Charles is operating at level 5 in his mathematics, in a class in which most children are at level 3, will Charles continue to show high ability in mathematics? Predictive validity can only really be determined with hindsight, i.e. when we know that Charles has or has not continued in the way predicted. Nevertheless, making predictions does form part of what teachers do, although there is a great danger that predictions can become self-fulfilling. We must not allow our early judgements to significantly affect our subsequent teaching responses, or those of others.

Labelling is probably the most damaging and reprehensible thing teachers do to children. If you do not consider it so, reflect on your own schooldays. You can probably still remember how hurtful it was to be earmarked as the child who could (or could not) do something; especially now that you can see how misguided that label may have been.

Construct validity   This has to do with the real understanding that a child may have. We all know about the tests and examinations that can be tackled through memorising facts. We should, though, be concerned with the extent to which the outcomes of assessment identify real understanding rather than superficial recall.

Handling marks and grades

In order to interpret and use different sorts of assessment it is necessary to look at how marks or grades must be handled. We need to know something about the statistical principles in order to avoid misinterpreting or misusing marks or grades we might attach to children's work.

Scores and normal distribution

The distribution of marks and grades in norm-referenced tests is generally assumed to be closely related to a *normal distribution curve*, as shown in Figure 3.3.

To some extent this curve bears out our impressions that there are a few children with high ability, a few with low ability and the majority are average. Such distributions have been common for many years and most of us have been trained to view this distribution as being the reality of classrooms. Our experience also tells us that we meet classes which have two or more very different groups of children, and we have all said things like, 'My class this year is different from usual' or . . . 'better than last year' and so on. However, in order to appreciate fully the possibilities and limitations of using a normal distribution, it is necessary to look at averages and notions of deviation from an average.

Averages

We all make use of the idea of 'average' in everyday conversations and observations. When we buy shoes we are used to the way they are sized and the fact that there are gaps between sizes – and it sometimes seems that our feet would be more comfortable in shoes that lie between sizes! In school we often talk about the average six-year-old, or an average class. In newspapers and magazines we read the results of surveys of the type which state that 'Most people prefer . . .'. In fact these everyday encounters illustrate that the term 'average' is liable to be used in different ways in different situations. The shoe manufacturer and the newspaper survey writer are both concerned with how many people there are in a category. If most women have a foot size which is close to a five, then that is the shoe size to make in greater quantity. There are, in fact, three sorts of average we can employ: mean, mode and median. Of these sorts of average, the mode is usually associated with categories and the mean and median are commonly associated with actual numerical quantities.

The mode   This is the average of the shoe manufacturer and is little used in assessment

Figure 3.3 Normal distribution

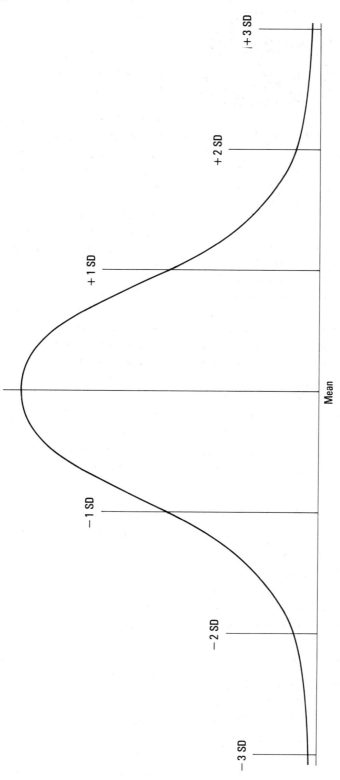

95% of people prefer Friskas

in a formal way. However, there is regular informal use of the idea of modal average. When you or your colleagues say things like 'Most of the children in my class are independent readers' the notion of the mode is being employed. Modal average is the most frequent: that which occurs most often. Its use in National Curriculum terms will come when attempts are made to draw a picture of the general trend in a year group. 'Most of the class are at level 3' is a modal statement. For example, imagine you were looking at science AT2 and had established the following pattern for 12 children who had been working on this particular attainment target:

Level 3 5 5 3 4 3 4 4 4 3 4 4

The modal average for this group would be level 4 as there are six occurrences compared with four at level 3 and two at level 5. In other words, the category to which most of the children belong is labelled level 4. The use of modal averages is limited, but they will be part of the repertoire of the teacher carrying out National Curriculum assessments.

The mean   This is the average with which most people are familiar. It is the average taught to most of us in our mathematics and science. The mean average is the average which is calculated by summing a set of scores and dividing by the number of scores in the

original list. Take the following marks for 30 children:

37	61	42	50	50	72	43	51	62
52	45	53	53	53	65	47	54	55
55	55	56	65	48	56	57	57	68
58	58	59						

The sum total is 1637, and with 30 contributing marks the mean average is 1637 ÷ 30, which equals 54.6 (rounded up to one decimal place), although no child got that exact score; this is often the case with mean averages.

Whilst 'mean' average is the one with which we commonly associate the word 'average', it is also the average which is most commonly misused. This misuse occurs in two ways:

● By the use of this averaging technique when modes or medians would be better
● By combining scores which are not actually amenable to combination without preliminary manipulation (see standardised scores on page 44).

The median   The median is the middle value of a set of marks. If there is an even number of marks, then the median will lie half-way between the two central marks.

4   5   5   7   7   8   9
            ↑

The median here is 7.

3   5   5   7   8   8
            ↑

The median here is 6.

1   3   4   4   4   4   9
            ↑

The median here is 4.

The median has an important use, for in a set of scores where there are one or two extreme scores which skew the mean average, the median can offer a better feel for the group achievement. There are two other areas in which using the median can be useful. These are:

- When you wish to get a feel for something without being able to collect the data you would need to use the mean
- When you want to report the relative position of a child in relation to his or her peers, whether by class or across classes within an age range.

Here is an example of how a median is used. One of the concerns that we all have is the time it takes for individual children to complete a given task. Investigations of the type being used for Standard Assessment Tasks are examples where there is a need to appraise the time taken on tasks. Using the median can be a useful way of getting a feel for the amount of time a particular task might take. To do so it is necessary for the teacher to observe the children, keeping a record of the time, and to register when the 'middle' child finishes. Then, even if time runs out before all the children can finish, you will have some data which will give you a very good idea of the overall time needed in the future. For example, 15 children took the following number of minutes to complete a task:

10 12 14 18 23 24 24 26 27
29 29 32 33 33 35

The median is 26 minutes and the mean is 24.6 minutes. If the time available had only been half an hour then four children would not have finished and it would not be possible to calculate the mean. But the median is available within the time, and is quite a good indicator of the 'average' time needed for the task.

In your own classroom it may be difficult to collect this information for as many as 15 children, but you can apply the same procedure, letting a smaller sector of the class do a task. With subsequent groups or classes you will then have an approximate idea about how much time to allow.

There are, then, some uses for medians (and for modes), but the reason that the mean is most commonly used is that it is less variable than the median. We will now look at further developments of ideas in relation to the mean.

Standard deviation

Recently some children at Smith Avenue Junior School, Townsville were given marks for their work in English and mathematics. Wesley received 55% for English and 75% for mathematics. Dora got 70% and 60% respectively for her English and maths. If we were to 'average' these results Wesley would get 65% overall and Dora would also get 65%: the same – or are they? In order to combine marks and interpret them we actually need more information. Looking at the class results we find that:

English	mean average for class 55%
Mathematics	mean average for class 60%

Further, if we calculate the range of deviations (a sample calculation follows on page 44) from the mean for each subject we find that for the whole class:

	Mean %	Standard Deviation
English	55	5
Mathematics	60	15

This indicates that the spread of marks in English is much lower (deviation 5) than in mathematics, where the standard deviation is 15. These facts will allow us to re-examine Wesley's and Dora's results.

Looking at English first, we see that Wesley's score of 55% is the class average, whereas Dora has a score which is 15 above the class average (three standard deviations). In mathematics Wesley's score of 75% is one standard deviation away from the class average whilst Dora's is on the average score. In order to compare the results we should think about the deviations away from the mean average. A convenient way of doing this is to take the original scores and the different standard deviations and fit them to a *standardised score*. To do this we need to work out how far from the mean average the scores are and then locate them a similar distance from a standard average and deviation. For example, if we adjust the marks for Wesley and Dora to a standardised average of 50 and a deviation of 10 we obtain the following results:

	English	Mathematics	Overall average
Wesley	50 (55)	60 (75)	55 (65)
Dora	80 (70)	50 (60)	65 (65)

The numbers in brackets are the original scores and the other numbers are the standardised scores. They look very different, and now we can see that it is Dora who has actually done rather better overall, and it is not as close as we had thought! In reflecting on this simple example it is important to keep in mind that in adjusting Wesley's and Dora's scores all we have done is to standardise them. We have kept the original deviations from the mean of the same order. In other words, this is not a fiddle!

A cautionary note Our example above shows the need to be statistically accurate. It takes no note of the way in which the scores were arrived at. The ways in which marking is carried out and judgements made are not amenable to statistical analysis in the way that raw scores are. In other words if you know that Wesley performs at a higher standard than Dora all round, then look at the way in which the scores are being arrived at. If you are going to 'average' results though, you really must look at adding like with like, and the use of standardisation applies. It is worth noting here that bought-in tests will (or

should) contain notes about their standardisation procedures. Most intelligence tests and many reading tests are based upon a mean of 100 and a standard deviation of 15. An example of how to compute standard deviations is given below.

Here is a set of science marks for 15 children. The marks are out of 20.

Marks	Deviation from the mean	Square of these deviations
3	−7.4	54.76
5	−5.4	29.16
7	−3.4	11.56
8	−2.4	5.76
9	−1.4	1.96
9	−1.4	1.96
10	−0.4	0.16
11	+0.6	0.36
11	+0.6	0.36
12	+1.6	2.56
12	+1.6	2.56
13	+2.6	6.76
14	+3.6	12.96
14	+3.6	12.96
18	+7.6	57.76
156		Sum = 201.6

$$\text{Mean} = \frac{156}{15} = 10.4$$

We now calculate the mean average of the squares of the deviations from the mean. This is known as the *variance* and is the mean of the sum of the squares of the deviations. To obtain the standard deviation we then take the square root of the variance.

$$\text{Variance} = \frac{201.6}{15} = 13.44$$

$$\text{Standard Deviation} = \sqrt{13.44} = 3.666$$

The results of the science test have a mean of 10.4 and a standard deviation of 3.666. Thus any child with a score of between about 7 and 14 (one standard deviation either side of the mean) is very close to the average performance.

Those who have scores below 7 or above 14 have done significantly worse or better, and those who have scores of 3 or below or 18 or above (approximately 3 standard deviations from the mean) have considerable problems, or have excellent understanding of the items within the test. In this case there are about 10 children within one standard deviation of the mean and there is one child with a score of 3 and one child with 18.

One of the outcomes of using means and standard deviations is the appreciation of children's achievements in relation to each other. This is a ranking procedure but one that is based upon the idea of a normal distribution curve (see Figure 3.3). There are other ways of ranking which are based on other principles.

Other ranking issues

In athletics events two measures are commonly employed: time or distance, and position. Of these two measures the awards go to position. Whilst it is grand to obtain a world record, or improve on your personal best, the greatest acclaim is given to those who come first! Positions are not dependent on times. It does not matter whether you are beaten in a race by one hundredth or one tenth of a second, the fact is that you came second. Positional location is commonly known in education as ranking. Ranking does not have to map onto a normal distribution or any other kind of curve. If your ranking is based on a distribution curve then many individuals will have the same rank. This is not usual when people talk of positions in class!

This does not mean, however, that normally distributed scores are not used for ranking purposes. Take, for example, this set of 10 scores for a science test marked out of 20:

18 17 14 13 12 11 11 9 7 5

Visual examination will indicate that the mean average is about 12. In fact the mean is

11.7, the median is 11.5 and the mode 11. Examination also shows that the intervals between scores is not equal. It ranges from three (the difference between 17 and 14) to one (e.g. the difference between 12 and 11). For the purposes of ranking this does not matter: 18 is first and five is tenth, and the two scores of 11 would be ranked, in school, as tied sixth. Ranking takes no note of intervals. So, in the following range of ten scores for a mathematics test, we can see how ranking can actually mask important trends:

19 18 18 17 14 11 7 4 4 1

Here the mean is 11.3, the median 12.5 and the mode 18. The distribution is clearly quite different in kind from the first example, but ranking would still give a first and a tenth. So, in looking at ranks it is important to understand what the messages are, and what has been omitted.

The other issue raised by these examples is to do with relationships. If the children have the same position in both their science and mathematics tests then we might start to draw some conclusions about ability. But what if the positions were very different, and first in maths was tenth in science and vice versa? Or what if there was no discernible pattern? This takes us to a consideration of the final, fundamental item of statistics that we need to be aware of as teachers: the concept of correlation.

Correlations

It is not our intention to look at the computation of correlations here. Rather we are concerned with the concept of correlation and what it means to say that things are 'correlated.'

Correlations can be described in three ways: positive, negative and no correlation, and they can be described with varying degrees of confidence. Correlations can be calculated for scores or for ranks. In the first case the computation would be based on an assumption of a normal distribution and in the second a no distribution curve would be considered and the correlation would depend solely upon the relative comparisons between two or more sets of ranked data.

Positive correlations These arise where, in relation to scores or ranks, there is a clear positive relationship between a score or rank on one test and a score or rank on another. In other words, if someone scores 90 out of 100 on one test and 19 out of 20 on another there would appear to be a strong, positive correlation between the two scores. This is what it looks like diagrammatically. The figure is known as a scattergram.

Figure 3.4 Positive scattergram

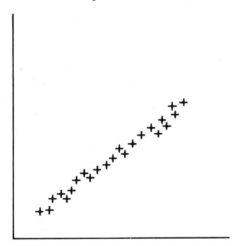

Negative correlations These are the converse of positive correlations. If, for example, the top ranked children in English were the bottom ranked in mathematics then there would be some evidence to suggest that the ranks were negatively correlated. Figure 3.5 shows a negative scattergram.

No correlation If there is no discernible connection between scores or ranks and the pattern produced is random then there is no correlation between the sets of data. This means that you cannot use one set of data to

Figure 3.5 Negative scattergram

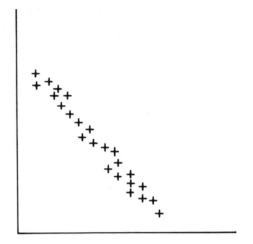

make any inferences about the other data in the way that you can with positively and negatively correlated data. This scattergram illustrates the situation.

Figure 3.6 No correlation scattergram

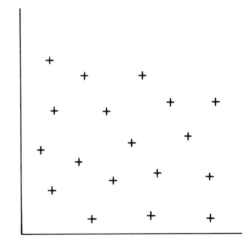

Degrees of confidence Looking at the scattergrams for positive and negative correlations it is easy to see that the closer the points form into a straight line the more certain you can be that there is a strong correlation between two sets of data. Conversely, the more scattered the less certain, and at some point no correlation would be discernible.

The notion of degrees of confidence can be found in mathematics AT14 where the central idea is that of locating events from impossible to absolutely certain. We all use these concepts of chance and correlation between events in everyday situations. We all predict outcomes on the basis of our experience and our prejudices! So if, for example, you decide to group children in ability groups based upon reading capability, and you keep them in those same groups for science, then you are implicitly asserting a correlation between reading and the ability to do science. What degree of confidence do you have? How do you know? When there appears to be a correlation between things and the correlations do not seem to make sense, we say that there are other hidden factors in between that are producing the correlation. These hidden factors are called intervening variables.

Summary

In this chapter we have discussed the purposes, language and principles of procedure in doing assessment. Whether an assessment is to have a summative, formative, diagnostic or evaluative use should determine the approach adopted and the possible kinds of judgements made about outcomes. Similar techniques can be used in different situations but they must fit the purpose for which the assessment is to be made.

We have described the main statistical principles upon which our assessment procedures are commonly based. We have done this for two reasons:

- All teachers must be aware of the possibilities and the constraints of data analysis, because they make judgements about children on the basis of this analysis
- All teachers need to be able to evaluate tests, whether they are of the reading test type or more thematic multi-task tests (like SATs), for they select and use such tests.

However, all of the knowledge offered in this chapter is of little consequence without real data with which to work. The next chapter looks at data collection methods and opportunities.

4

DOING ASSESSMENT

Due to a long tradition of testing within our educational system, which is rooted in ideas of the external, objective and standardised test, there is a common belief that assessment has to be 'scientific' in order to have validity. However, the strict application of scientific principles which call for the careful control of variables and require the capacity for repeats of the same experimental work are problematic in the real world of the school and classroom. It is neither possible nor desirable for us to pretend to have laboratory conditions when attempting to appraise the standards and progress of children. It is, however, necessary to approach the task of assessing children's progress with fairness and consistency.

To assess children's performance and potential, you need to be not only a researcher and report writer, but also the person who implements the outcomes of your research. However, in researching your own classroom you do not need to look and behave like a scientist. You are a participant and one of the main characters in the classroom drama, and as a principal actor, the way in which you deliver your lines and make your gestures affects the progress of the research and its outcomes. This is different from research in the strictly scientific tradition. There are, however, some aspects of method which scientists and teachers as assessors can share. These include:

- Clearly defining the scope of an enquiry
- Attempting to minimise the likelihood of biased results
- Careful interpretation of findings
- Accurate and succinct compilation of outcomes.

Many teachers already try to incorporate all these aspects into their assessment work, but it is now increasingly important for everyone in education to develop and hone their research skills, using features of a scientific approach only where it is useful. All the facets of method listed above are touched on in this book. There is a discussion of some aspects of bias in Chapter 3. You will find help in the presentation of outcomes in Chapter 5. This chapter will tell you much about sorting out what to assess, collecting information and making interpretations.

Identifying the pool of information

Many people seem to think that it is easy to identify what should be assessed in school. This may be because there are a number of rather broad labels, like 'knowledge' and 'aptitudes', which we use in conversation about schooling. These concepts are in fact complex and not always helpful in defining classroom assessment. For example, having inspected the National Curriculum Statutory

Orders, (which are mostly lists of knowledge items) a non-educationalist might say, 'Why don't you just test on every statement of attainment in every attainment target?' We know that even if that were what teachers thought necessary, it would be a far from straightforward task. To approach it in that way would overload the teacher with assessment jobs. So numerous are they, that he or she would not have the time to teach the very things on which his or her assessments might focus.

However, the question posed above does illustrate a misunderstanding that is common among people who have a limited view of assessment, and we feel it has flavoured the outcomes (though perhaps not the intent) of the TGAT and SEAC. The mistake is to assume that to be good, assessment has to cover everything. We would argue that assessment is not, and should not be, exhaustive; it does, however, need to include all the indicators necessary to make insightful judgements. Assessments are like the lines in an accurate sketch: though the picture is skeletal, all the important ingredients are there, and the added colours and detail are the interpretations made afterwards.

Of course we need to begin the process of defining what to assess by digesting the legislation to discover the minimum prescriptions for assessment. Then we need to carefully tease out the things we need to look for which are indicators of achievement. The information in the official documents does not transfer directly to the classroom. Quite apart from the sheer volume of data available, if you choose to use the Statutory Orders by saying: 'I am going to assess this group on these statements of attainment, at level N from ATs X and Y today', this does not demonstrate what you have chosen as the exact data you need to make judgements, nor how you are going to collect it.

We offer a solution to this problem. Our starter question was 'What are the kinds of information accessible to teachers as assessors?' The answer is that they have available to them all the kinds of things children do when they are working in school.

What children do in school

If we disregard all the conventional ways of describing children's schoolwork, including subjects, activities, sessions, tasks, experiences, etc. we can then look for a general way of grouping the things children do. These need not be tied to subject or session, but they will still be 'assessable'.

On close examination, what children actually do when they are working in school falls into seven categories. These are not quite mutually exclusive, but we have chosen them because we think they are directly transferable to working classrooms, and they do provide a strategy for coping with the deluge of data in a non-technical way.

CATEGORIES OF WORK

- Oral/aural

- Reading

- Practical

- Written

- Research

- Co-ordination and control

- Aesthetic

Overleaf are some examples of the kinds of things that children do which fit each of the categories.

Oral/aural   Speaking clearly, using a wide vocabulary, listening, questioning, answering, following instructions

Reading   Getting meaning from the printed word, reading for pleasure

Practical (Doing/experimenting)   Assembling the necessary equipment, carrying out observations, making things happen, modifying the action, carrying the task through

Written   Forming letters correctly, recording what has happened, what might happen, what is happening, messages (including poems, feelings, lists), 'answers'

Research (Finding out/reflecting)   From people, from non-fiction and fiction books and other sources such as pamphlets, posters and TV

Co-ordination and control   Writing evenly, handling scissors and brushes, ball skills, dance

Aesthetic   Visual communication using paint, collage, sculpture and display. Making music, dance and drama

Methods for collecting assessment information

To sort out all the methods of data collection that teachers might profitably use, we have taken each of the categories of 'things children do' and posed the question, 'How can the teacher collect information about this?' Figure 4.1 (see opposite) shows the outcome of 'matching' children's work to ways the teacher may get to know about it.

As you can see, the number of methods of information collection appropriate for the teacher is quite small. There are five in all.

METHODS OF COLLECTING INFORMATION

- Observing
- Listening
- Participating
- Scrutinising written outcomes
- Giving tests

We shall spell out how to do each of these in turn, pointing out some of the strengths and difficulties you may find in each method. Our intention is to alert you to possible approaches, and to the rigour necessary in being a professional assessor.

Observation skills for teachers

To confine your observation is a skill. Many teachers, of necessity, have the amazing capacity to notice several events at the same time. This is a creditable asset, except when you are assessing. It is then that you have to ensure that the partial information you have, on the basis of your observation, is adequate for making judgements. If you are watching the argument over books in the reading corner, the progress of the work on number bonds to 20 at the maths table, and the cutting and sticking skills of the children at the painting table, it may be that you miss Ellen's attempts to arbitrate in the book dispute (social development), Oscar's powers of computation in maths (maths AT3, level 3) and Pam's reliance on Lucy to do her cutting for her (basic co-ordination and hand control). You will need practice and support to become an expert observer.

How to observe

Before you start:

- Decide what it is that you are going to observe. The clearer you are about exactly

Figure 4.1 Assessment information collection

WHAT CHILDREN DO IN SCHOOL	HOW THE TEACHER CAN COLLECT INFORMATION
Oral/aural	Observe, listen, participate
Reading	Observe, listen, participate, give a test
Practical	Observe, listen, participate, scrutinise written outcomes, give a 'multi-task' test
Written	Scrutinise outcomes, give a test
Research	As for practical
Co-ordination and control	Observe, scrutinise outcomes (for example handwriting, model-making, swimming), give a test
Aesthetic	Observe, listen, scrutinise outcomes (for example drawings, paintings, models)

what it is you are looking for, the more likely you are to notice it!

● Arrange the class and groupings so that you can sit in view, but unobtrusively. As far as the children are concerned, and that includes the child or children you are observing, it should be business as usual. Do not be tempted, therefore, to sit in the stock cupboard, or behind the blackboard, unless you commonly do it anyway, for the children will respond by 'abnormal' behaviour too.

While the class is in progress:

● Sit and concentrate
● Take chronological notes of what you see; the notes will be incident-related
● Do not leave things out of your notes, unless they are really irrelevant.

After the class:

● Sift and summarise your notes
● Make interpretations and record assessments.

Overleaf, Figure 4.2 is a suggested layout for an observation form.

Figure 4.2 Observation form: suggested layout

DATE	TIME
Name(s) of child(ren)	
Work assigned	
What happened	
Comments	
Contribution to assessment of:	

Advantages

- Observation is the only method for assessing much of the work that children do, while it is going on
- It is a good method for gleaning a range of information during one session about an individual child, or a group of children.

Shortcomings

- It can require narrow focusing and total concentration

- It needs support to organise, preferably another adult in the room
- It is not good for one-off assessments, for the very thing you have decided to observe may not happen while you are looking on.

Listening skills for teachers

Really focusing your listening is a skill. Many teachers (and many children) cultivate the image that they are good listeners, while their

52

thoughts are elsewhere. Teachers are also under pressure to monitor, by listening to several things at once. A teacher may find him or herself, for example, trying to hear what is happening out in the bay (by the sound level), how well Sian is reading while standing alongside him or her, and whether the class survey, entitled 'Foods we like', is amassing the right sort of information. Some of your listening assessments can, however, be made while most of the children are listening too. This may happen, for example, when there is an improvised puppet play presented by the children, or one child reads to the class, or they are giving their 'news' or sharing funny memories. Other kinds of listening will (just like observation) require practice and support.

Figure 4.3 Listening form: suggested layout

DATE	TIME	
Name(s) of child(ren)		
Work assigned		
Initials of Child	Notes on what was said	Context
Comments		
Contribution to assessment of:		

How to listen

Before you start:

- Decide whether your focus is on what the child says to you, or to other children while working, or to an audience, which may range from a group to the class or even the whole school
- Amend the timetable so that you can listen; in other words, arrange activities, where appropriate, to ensure quiet.

While the class is in progress:

- Concentrate
- Take notes, or use a tape recorder.

After the class:

- Use your notes and tape to make interpretations and add to records. (There are comments on using a tape recorder later in the chapter).

Figure 4.3 on page 53 shows one way of setting down what you hear, when listening to assess.

Advantages

- Though listening requires concentration, you can do it for a short while to good effect
- You can make the content relevant in discussion with an individual child
- Serendipity is possible, for you can hear by chance, even when you are not listening!

Shortcomings

- It is tempting to interrupt; be sensitive to the flow and try to prevent 'talk' being stopped too soon
- It can be difficult to maintain sustained concentration
- You need to guard against premature or inaccurate interpretation.

Participation skills for teachers

Joining in can change the action, and the teacher should try to avoid there being a bias in, for example, the outcome of an experiment some children are doing, because of his or her participation. We do not mean that you should not help children do experiments, but it is patently wrong to participate so often that they can only do experiments successfully if you help. When you decide to join in an activity which you wish to assess, you do need to ensure that you know why you are participating rather than observing and/or listening.

How to participate

Before you start:

- Decide who and what are to be the subjects of your judgements
- Place yourself at the heart of the action, and arrange that there will not be demands on you from another part of the room.

While the class is in progress:

- Be realistic about the scope of your assessment in one session
- Join in without dominating
- Keep your contributions to the minimum, while still being a 'member' of the group
- Offer choices of action and ask questions such as 'What do you think would happen if . . . ?' and 'What other ways could you try it?'
- Avoid closing options such as 'Let's do it this way . . .', 'There are no other answers, are there?', '. . . Surely there's no point in doing that again!'

After the class:

- As soon as possible, write something down
- Interpret the points of interest that you noted
- Compile records.

Figure 4.4 Participation form: suggested layout

DATE	TIME	
Name(s) of child(ren)		
What the child(ren) did		What I did
Comments		
Contribution to assessment of:		

A possible way of writing down what happens when you participate is shown above in Figure 4.4.

Advantages

● It does not need to be as contrived as the use of some other methods, and you can do it 'naturally'.

Shortcomings

● It is difficult to focus on specific information for assessment while you are 'in the thick of it'
● Opportunities to write things down, or to make use of a tape recorder may be limited

● It is tempting to do too much for the children and force the pace of activity
● Beware of changing the direction of learning to fit in with your own predictions, unless you are sure the children are getting nowhere.

Teachers' skills in scrutinising written work and drawings

Written work Once children can write, their written work becomes the basic material that teachers use to make assessments. It is also used by the children and their parents as an index of progress. Many children do not think they have done any work unless they have written something down, and parents are often more impressed by how many exercise books their child has filled at the end of the year than by their own or your perceptions of their children's progress. Because written work is ubiquitous in school, there are a great variety of things that are assessable about it. These include:

- Skills such as letter formation, use of upper and lower case letters and punctuation
- Quality and quantity of content, whether that is creative or factual
- Construction, grammar, order and flow of the writing
- Presentation, including whether the style is appropriate and neat.

Many children write so much that their teachers could not possibly assess every piece. It is important that children's work is seen and marked by their teacher, but for 'scrutinisation' you need to sample children's work. Doing this with each child present is the ideal situation. Then the assessment can be really formative, for the child will know about your expectations and what you are 'looking for' in their work; they will know which things they did well, and how they can make progress. You will have the assessment data still available, and written evidence of your judgements. Of course, neither you nor the children have the time to do all written work assessment this way. It has to be timetabled in for you to be able to do it occasionally. Other assessment of written work has to be done out of school hours. Even when assessing children's work in their absence, you still have the problem of 'noise'. Here we mean those aspects of the children's work that we need to exclude from the assessment, but which may distract us and skew our judgement. Imagine, for example, that you are presented with a similar piece of work from two different children, and you wish to assess only the content of the work. If one piece is easy to read and well presented, while the other is untidy and almost illegible, you would need to try not to let presentation colour your judgement. The key, therefore, in assessing written work, is to focus only on what you have decided to assess, and to avoid contamination of your judgements. This includes contamination by your own ideas and preferences about style and what represents creative effort.

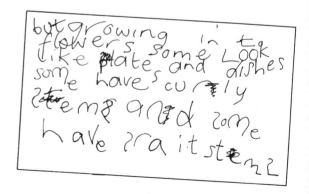

There are formal external writing tests available. In our experience they have not been in common use in primary schools. If you feel such a test is appropriate, and that it will augment your own judgements, consult the section on tests later in this chapter.

Drawings Assessment of work in which aesthetic sense is a major component is probably hardest of all; it is also impossible to avoid. Whether or not you intend to judge children's decisions about the use of colour, tone, etc. they do affect your assessments. Much of what we have said about written work also applies to drawings. These are ubiquitous, particularly before children become skilled writers, and there is much that can be assessed about them. The aspects for assessment (as with written work) include:

● Skills such as mixing a desired colour
● Quality and quantity of content, including aesthetic elements and insertion of detail
● Construction, including composition and whether the work corresponds with a developmental phase for the child
● Presentation, including style and 'neatness'.

How to scrutinise written work and drawings

Before you start:

● Decide what it is you are going to assess; you could, for example, go though one piece of work assessing it for all the assessable features listed above
● Decide how often you need to sample a particular child's work, and if and when you will be able to do the assessing in consultation with them.

Whether in or out of class:

● Make sure the marks you make on work mean the same to you as to the children
● Take the time to do it properly; the effect of skimped time may be that the child will feel

that you consider the work (and therefore him or her) to be of little importance.

While the class is in progress:

● Let the child whose work you are assessing stand by you so that you can discuss the work (otherwise there is no justification for assessing written work in class)
● Explain to the child exactly what you are looking for.

After the class:

● Make judgements and put them on record.

The written work or drawing itself is your first stage of data collection, and you can write on or under it the notes and interpretations you make. If you wish to have a separate record from children's work, you may like to try setting out your comments on forms such as those in Figures 4.5 and 4.6 (see pages 58 and 59).

Advantages

● You can assess written work and drawings when the children are not there
● The assessment data is concrete and available to you whenever you want it.

Shortcomings

● Your personal taste can affect your interpretations.

Teachers' skills in giving tests

The greatest skill you need in giving tests is to stick exactly to the rules. 'Bought-in' tests and those required as part of National Curriculum assessment will have accompanying notes about the following:

● Setting up arrangements, for example, whether children must work alone or can consult, how long is required for the test and so on

Figure 4.5 Written work assessment analysis

NAME	TASK		
	COMMENTS		
Content			
Grammar			
Spelling			
Style appropriate for context? for audience?			
'Quality' Aesthetic/ creative aspects			
Marks/grades if appropriate			
Overview			

- Administering the test, for example, whether it has more than one version, how to take children through practice questions, the form of words to use in talking to the children before and during the test, and so on
- Marking the test, for example, rules for marking, how to combine marks using weighting and so on

- Interpreting the marks, for example, the conversion of raw scores to standardised scores, and what final scores mean.

If you devise tests yourself, and this includes tests of spelling, mental arithmetic and other 'five minute' quick tests you may do regularly, you do need to be aware of a number of principles. Much of what is said in Chapter 3

Figure 4.6 Art assessment analysis

NAME	TASK	
	COMMENTS	
Technical skills		
Observation		
Investigation (colour, texture, etc.)		
Communication		
Self-assurance		
Overview		

will alert you to possible problems. The questions to ask yourself are:

- Is a test the best way to assess this? For example, you may get a better idea about children's spelling skills through scrutinising written work and then targeting 'poor' spellers with remediation
- Is this test appropriate for all the children who will do it?
- Does the test *really* assess what I think it does? For example, do spelling tests show memory or word-building skills?
- Is my marking fair?
- Are my interpretations correct?

Both 'bought-in' tests and tests you have devised yourself can be of various kinds. As a teacher you need to know about the different sorts so that you may choose an appropriate test. Tests may be done by the whole class, by groups within it, or by individuals.

Group tests: whole class These have been in widespread use in many local authorities since the inception of the 11+ examination. Prior to the introduction of the National Curriculum they were used by local authorities as the main way of pressing schools into measuring performance.

The advantages in these kinds of test are that they are often easy to administer during a normal school day, and easy to score; they also give an idea of ability range. Their disadvantages lie in their specificity, tied in with the wording of the test items and their layout, and the fact that they give little individual feedback.

Group tests: co-operative   There is a flurry of interest in this kind of test, for it is the kind being tried for National Curriculum assessment purposes. Typically these are multi-task tests where the intention is that children demonstrate what they know through action and interaction, both by doing practical activity together, and by recording outcomes. Standard Assessment Tasks take the form of group tests. They carry the advantages that several areas of learning can be worked on in the assessment situation, they are less artificial than some tests, and they attempt to look at processes as well as products of learning. The disadvantages are that they make great demands on the teacher doing the assessing in terms of expertise, time and management, and they are subject to the unpredictable effects of children's personalities on one another, through their attitudes and what they say and do.

Individual tests   These are in widespread use for diagnostic purposes and for young children whose reading and writing skills are limited. They are advantageous in being potentially more wide-ranging or thorough and offering more feedback on specific areas of performance. Their difficulties lie in the fact that they are extremely demanding in terms of time, and are wholly impractical in a classroom setting, for they require a one-to-one situation for administration.

Whether they are designed for groups or individual children, tests vary tremendously

in the way they are set out. Following are some of the different types of written test.

Multiple choice   In these tests children have to select the correct answer to each question from the range offered. Multiple-choice tests can cover a considerable range of subject matter and they are easy to mark. However, they cannot be used for testing real 'understanding', for children's scores can reflect recall and question comprehension. You can invent multiple-choice tests yourself for testing factual learning, but remember to be sensitive to the possible bias in the wording of questions and answers. Some examples of multiple-choice test items include:

$$10 \times 12 = ? \qquad 200$$
$$120$$
$$22$$

Foot is to shoe as hand is to?   hat
                                     shake
                                     glove

True/false and yes/no   These are fun to do, and can make tests less stressful. They are easy to administer, for they are either written for the children to read at their own pace, or the teacher reads them out. They are also easy to mark. However, they do not provide the children with the opportunity to offer modified or creative answers such as: 'True but only when . . .' They also assume that everyone has the same understanding of the question. Here are some examples:

A quadrilateral is any four-sided figure   True/False

The Moon is a star   True/False

Poetry always rhymes   True/False

Comprehension The two main kinds of comprehension 'test' in use in primary classrooms are sentence provision and sentence completion. In sentence provision tests, children are given a written passage and a set of questions which they then answer in writing. This is a test of understanding and interpretation. These are easy to set and to mark, but are rather tedious for children to do.

Here is an example:

Mr Greengage always bought the paper on the way to work. One Monday morning, however, he found no papers at the news-stand. Instead, a tersely worded official notice read, "Due to world paper shortage, it has been decided that newspapers will be discontinued until more trees grow. By order, Ministry of Communications." Mr Greengage was outraged. Not only was he to be deprived of something to read on the way to work, but no longer would he smell the aroma of printers' ink and have the pleasure of using the industrial cleaner he kept in his desk drawer to get it off his hands.

What did Mr Greengage buy on the way to work?
When did he find no papers at the news-stand?
Which Ministry was responsible for the message about the paper stoppage?

If part answers are provided for the children to complete (sentence completion), then their understanding, vocabulary and grammar are often given 'scores'. Sentence completion tests can be more motivating for children, but scores are heavily dependent on the tester's interpretations of what constitutes an appropriate answer.

Cloze procedure is a kind of sentence completion comprehension exercise. A written passage with a word omitted at regular fixed intervals, perhaps every fifth or seventh word, is given to the children. The children have to fill those gaps. This is a way of testing understanding, grammar and sentence construction, but it is time-consuming to mark and really does demand some consultation with the child about what is 'correct' or appropriate.

Here is an example of cloze procedure:

Nell closed the book ____ she had been reading, ____ was quite the ____ exciting book she had ____ read. It had all ____ things that you expect ____ good stories, like a ____ , a princess and a ____ .

Some possible words which would fit the gaps are: that, Here, most, ever, the, in, dragon, wizard.

How to test

With a 'bought-in' or nationally prescribed test, you need to fully understand how to set up, administer, score and interpret the test, and then do *exactly* as the manual tells you. Misuse of a test may invalidate the results. You also need to be able to say:

- Why you test (it may be that the head-teacher, local authority or the law makes it mandatory)
- Why you use the particular test(s) chosen
- What scores mean.

If you have devised a test yourself, and you are convinced it meets all the exacting standards you now apply to tests of that sort, then you can devise the best ways to administer it, mark and interpret results. You also need to be able to say:

- Why you test
- Why you test in that way
- What scores mean.

Advantages

- Many tests are easy to administer and do not carry the management problems of some other assessment methods.

Shortcomings

- Test results cannot be generalised; they are test specific. If a child does well on one test, it does not mean he or she will do well on another
- Test results are often performance overviews and can give little indication of specific problems or strengths
- Test results are not good predictors of future performance and cannot be used in comments on potential.

Devices and skills to aid assessment

There are a number of ways in which you can extend your own repertoire of skills to help you when you are observing, listening and participating in class.

Diaries and logs

Diaries and logs are particularly good for collecting open-ended information and pin-pointing problems or strengths in classroom learning processes over time. If, for example, some children consistently do less well than you expect in some part of the curriculum or on a particular day of the week, you need to find out, over time, why this is so. Firstly, decide for how long you will keep the diary. You need to hazard a guess as to when you will have enough information to make judgements. It may be that you make diary notes on four consecutive Tuesdays, or every afternoon for a fortnight, or straight after PE for half a term. They may be notes of what you have seen or heard, but what is also important to write down is when these things happened. Your notes can be cryptic, full sentences, or spoken onto tape. You are the only person to make the first set of judgements, so the notes only need to communicate something to you.

Using a tape recorder

Tape recordings for your own use can be made in situations when you do not have the opportunity to write anything down. You do need good quality equipment, and it may still prove difficult to hear what is happening, for the recording will pick up all the background noise that we tend to ignore when we are listening to people talking. Try to listen to the tape as soon as you can after the recording, or you may forget what unspoken things were going on. Do not rely on your ability to transcribe material for record purposes – it takes too long.

Tape recordings are particularly good in these situations:

- Personal 'notes' when you have no opportunity to write anything down
- Assessing children's communication skills
- Self-assessment by children.

Extract from a diary

> Diary Wed. p.m. Art sessions Gps 3 and 4
>
> 7/11 Efforts did not meet my expectations. Some weak cutting skills. Look at cutting skills and weights etc. of materials. More practice necessary. More structured tasks'? Break up group?
>
> 14/11 Cutting and plaiting—much co-operative activity. Need to watch pairing to see that children mutually supportive.
>
> 21/11 Excellent session - v. small groups, children stimulated, rest of class busy. I was able to give time to 'artists' clay, painting and plaiting with splendid results. Started art display.
>
> 28/11 Plaiting, clay, crayon and shakers. Many children did all four - good idea?

Asking questions

Teachers regularly ask questions to assess what children know. It is probable that few teachers view their own ways of asking questions with the same critical air that they apply to tests or other assessment techniques. We do need to be as vigilant about bias in asking questions as in using any other strategy for assessment. For example, if we ask questions that are 'closed' (i.e. requiring 'yes' or 'no' answers), we give children little opportunity to be more expansive; 'What else . . . what other things . . . what other ways . . ?' are more encouraging than 'Anything else?' and even more so than 'Nothing else?'

We use informal questioning during the course of conversation all the time in the classroom. For assessment purposes, this is an important part of your participation technique. It is important to remember that the child who always answers may not be the only one who knows all the answers! Also you can make no assumptions about the achievement of the children who were not asked or did not answer.

If you wish, you can use more formal questioning. This can be done orally, through interviews, or in writing, using questionnaires. If you are using them for assessment, they really are home-devised 'vivas' or written tests for which the children have not necessarily prepared. As with informal questions, the wording in interviews and on questionnaires needs to be carefully worked out. Remember not to read too much into the results of such tests, for they have not been validated.

Group discussions

With the increase in group work in the primary school, these are now common in classrooms as well as in the staffroom. There are several ways of setting up discussions which would contribute information to your broad assessments. Discussions are particularly good at providing information to fuel your plans for 'next steps' and future work for a group. Most importantly they permit contributions from reticent children. They also motivate children if they are used infrequently enough to remain novel. Methods include maps, 'snowball' and nominal group technique.

Maps   For example, children can be asked to 'map' all the ideas they have about a topic onto a web. This information may help you to decide the course of future topic work. (See example below.)

Snowball   Using a snowball, ask the children to write or draw their ideas on a topic: for example , 'Things I am afraid of', 'What makes a book "good"?' or 'Friends'. Then get them to talk quietly to a classmate about their ideas. Next, place the pairs in larger groups. Finally, draw all the contributions into a class session.

A young child's map of day and night with words dictated to the teacher and written in by her

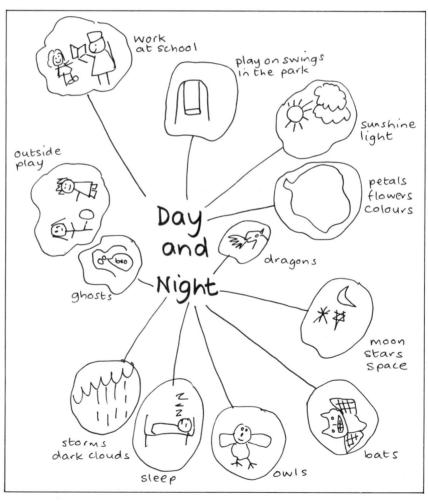

Nominal group technique   In nominal group technique you need an issue which can be polarised: for example, 'Likes and dislikes about school'. On the blackboard or a big sheet of paper, write or draw all the 'likes', taking one from each child until there are no more new ideas. Then do the same for 'dislikes'. The resulting lists can provide your starting point for a school survey or a project entitled 'The school my great grandad went to', 'School in the year 3000', or 'Alternatives to school'.

Limits to your choice of assessment method

So far our contention has been that you are at liberty to choose the assessment method which you feel most appropriate to assist the judgements you are going to be making. We know that teachers are under considerable pressures which will sometimes limit that range of choice. Amongst these pressures, the most important are those from the audiences for your assessments. Children and parents may want to know their 'scores'. The head-teacher may ask for 'results' that are publish-able, in accordance with the recommendations and requirements of the Law. Your colleagues may ask you for summary tick sheets that they can add to. There is more discussion of these dilemmas in Chapter 5. You are also restricted by having limited resources. To do assessment well demands sophisticated planning and sensitive, creative use of the resources available to you. This is the subject of Chapter 6.

Carrying through assessment

With an understanding of what assessment data is, a bank of methods to choose from and a realisation of the factors which can limit our choice of method, we can now look at the processes involved in carrying an assessment through.

STEPS IN MAKING AN ASSESSMENT

1 What is the assessment of?

2 What is the assessment for?

3 What resources are needed?

4 What do the children actually do?

5 What information do I need to collect?

6 How am I going to collect it?

7 How shall I collate the information?

8 What are the possible judgements I can make?

9 What shall I do with the outcomes?

10 What happens after this assessment?

Interpreting findings

Teachers' judgements are no less worthwhile than external test scores, providing they are, as far as possible, without bias. You make many assessment judgements throughout the school term, and to avoid bias in these is a constant self-evaluation exercise.

Before settling on an interpretation or judge-ment, consider whether:

- You collected appropriate information
- You collected enough information
- For criterion-referenced judgements, factors other than the task itself did not (as far as possible) affect the child's performance
- For norm-referenced judgements, the task was presented in the same way as for other children, and in accordance with the specific conditions set down for the test.

When you have made a judgement you should be able, if required, to spell out the reasons for that judgement. Your reasons, if they were set down in writing, might look something like the examples shown overleaf.

Alana's answers to my questions indicate that she knows about fractions.

or

Alana's answers to the fraction problems in her book show me that she knows about fractions and that she can provide correct answers.

I have seen Valerie catch a ball many times in games.

I have seen Leanne read a thermometer correctly on several occasions.

Rob can understand and follow instructions because I have heard him explain what to do to other children in his group about a dozen times in the last month.

I have seen Chris use his table of results in deciding how to set up his next experiment.

To make a model like this, Ruth must know about gears and how to build them out of junk materials in robust fashion.

I know Richard can explain his thinking because when I was working with him he said, 'When this ball goes in the water ... will happen because ... the next boat I make will be different from the one I have just made in these ways ... and I would change it because ...'

Attitudes and assessment

In this chapter we have focused on what children do in school rather than their approach to it, their manner of doing it or their attitudes to it. Inevitably, as teacher assessor these things will affect your judgements. It is quite proper that they should. We are working with whole people, not automatons, and we should be rightly concerned about children whose attitudes and orientations adversely affect their work.

The word 'attitudes' is often used as a catch-all to embrace all those parts of a child's personality which may impinge on learning. These include things such as feelings about school and learning, motivation, perseverance, ability to attend and concentrate, time keeping, interests and ambitions, confidence and self-image.

Teachers of young children have a major contribution to make, not only in the assessment of attitudes but also in the modification of them. We may all have taught children who have 'dropped out' by the time they are six. Our responsibilities go beyond assessing Shane as a no-hoper and a no-good. Those assessments must force us to evaluate our teaching programmes in order to re-engage Shane, if only instrumentally, so that he does not reduce his future options.

Summary

We have discussed the sorts of data that can be assessed and the possible range of methods of collection. At the heart of our concerns are the needs of children and the role held by assessment in meeting those needs. This is what is most important, regardless of the demands of any prescribed curriculum assessment, whether it is specifically devised or simply appropriated for such use. All of our futures depend upon the quality of educational opportunity offered to young people. Therefore, assessment *must* be regarded and evaluated in terms of the feedback and the messages it gives to children.

To carry through your assessments you will need to consider the audience for whom assessment outcomes are intended, and that is one of the themes of the next chapter (Chapter 5). You will also need adequate resources extending beyond your own personal expertise, and these are discussed in Chapter 6.

5

RECORDS AND REPORTS

Records and reports are communication devices. There can be little dispute about that. However, communication *about* records and reports is fraught with problems. These relate not only to the proposed intentions and audience for the documents, but also to their coverage and specific content. In fact, in many of the books available for teachers, the subject of record-keeping is dealt with very briefly. We believe that this is because talk about record-keeping is an issue which authors shy away from.

Some teachers do not get to grips with the problems there are in record-keeping either. They regard record-keeping as the tail-end of their job: the extra task that clouds a week or two at the end of the term or year. They may view records as the 'past preserved' and therefore take little notice of what is in them. They neither use them to form a frame of reference about children who are new to their class, nor to fuel future teaching and learning plans.

Why we keep records and make reports

In contrast to the attitudes mentioned above, we would argue that records and reports are indispensable documents which you can use in the following ways:

● To support your own memory

● To promote teamwork and common endeavour amongst colleagues in your school
● To foster continuity and progression between schools and local authorities
● To further understanding and co-operation with other professionals in meeting the needs of children
● To develop links between parents and schooling.

An inadequate record may not only be a sign that a teacher is not taking his or her assessment role seriously, but may also be an indication that children's achievements and potential do not matter to that teacher. In short, scrappy records may mean that the teacher simply does not care.

Having dispelled any myths that records are unimportant, we need to establish what goes into the records. In arguing so forcefully for adequate records, we do not necessarily mean *more* records. In Chapter 4 we suggest that, to be 'good', assessment does not need to cover all the work that children do. Assessments should be made on a sample of the children's work, and the resulting judgements should be sampled again for record purposes. Of course record-keeping is not more important than making judgements about children's learning, but those judgements are worthless unless they are communicated appropriately.

When we are thinking about devising 'good'

records, it helps to pin-point some of the things to be avoided. Here are some suggestions. School records should not be:

- "*A waste of teacher time*
- *Too jargonistic or too lengthy*
- *Used to check up on the work of the teacher*
- *A substitute for, or an addition to, gossip in the staffroom designed to transmit to a new teacher the opinions, impressions and prejudices of his/her predecessor*
- *Used as a bureaucratic device to increase the school's control over the lives of its pupils.*"

Clift, P. *et al., Record Keeping in Primary Schools*
(Macmillan Education, 1981) p. 23

Functions of school records and reports

There is a dearth of good analysis of record-keeping, but a notable exception is the work done in The Schools Council project reported in Clift, P. et al., cited above. The findings were that records are for teachers to:

- Keep information for their own use ('day-to-day')
- Pass on information within a school, to other teachers and to the headteacher ('summary')
- Hand on information when children are of an age to go onto the next formal stage ('transition')
- Send information when a child is moved to another school during a stage ('transfer')
- Pin-point educational problems or find out whether children are at risk ('diagnostic')
- Provide information for outside agencies such as the school doctor or psychologist ('welfare')
- Compile reports (for parents).

Distinguishing between records and reports

Differences of principle and content We view records as relatively flexible, on-going documents, with a built-in assumption that

they are 'unfinished' in the sense that they can be added to. Records are kept within a school (internal) and may be passed on from one school to another in their entirety. In contrast, reports are a special kind of record. They summarise or present partial information (sometimes gleaned from records) and they are commonly made at the end of a phase or stage of education, or at the end of a decision-making process (as in referrals). Referral reports for health, academic or other reasons can be made at any time, though there may be local regulations regarding timing. Reports to parents are often made at the end of a year, stage or phase. However, if reports take the form of a discussion or profile, they can have a formative as well as a summative purpose.

It seems to us that the principle behind a record is that it will not only be used as the basis for decisions, but that it will be added to, over time, with similar categories of information. In principle, reports present a 'case'; decisions have already been made by the teacher, and he or she is saying, 'Here is my judgement'. It is then for the recipient, for example, the school doctor, the educational psychologist or the parent, to evaluate the judgement, add their own expertise and act.

Different audiences Records and reports should be clear, succinct and apposite, whether they are for limited use within a school, or for a wider audience.

It is all the more imperative to make the record easy to understand when a child moves during a phase of his or her education, or moves from infant to junior school, or on to secondary school, because misunderstandings are harder to clear up once the child has moved.

National legislation, local authorities, employers, parents and even some teachers press for the use of more formal rather than informal methods of assessment. This affects

Part of a teacher devised record for science AT9 L2. Note that the activities are summarised, and details of assessment methods are not included, but colleagues would know that this child needs no further work on these S of A.

S of A Assessed ↓	Activities completed. ↓	Judgements made. ↓
weather and seasons ——— weather and people's lives	observation – all four seasons / recording in words and pictures weather calendar animals and the weather study ——— clothes / food / habits and weather	Good group of vocabulary, conceptual links between weather, the environment, people and animals. Complete mastery of these S of A. 20/9/90

the accompanying recording procedures. If the audience for whom a record or report is designed insists on marks and grades and sets great store by them, what is recorded will reflect this insistence. Judgements made by professionals working daily with children are squeezed out of such records, because of lack of space and their relative lack of value to the audience. If teachers make a concerted effort, those who view the assessments will come to value teachers' judgements as being more wide-ranging, holistic and therefore more realistic than the marks and grades that emerge from tests. Records and reports will then present more opportunities to point out real signs of the achievements and potential of children.

What is put on record

The range of information

We have pointed out elsewhere (Clemson, D. and Clemson, W. *The Really Practical Guide to National Curriculum 5-11.* 1989.) that all that teachers do in school has some form of record attached to it. Here are some typical examples:

- Who is on playground duty
- Parts of National Curriculum science programme of study tackled with 3B
- Which group uses the computer on Tuesdays
- The kind of regular medication that Maurice needs
- Which books Natalie is reading
- Who is absent from school.

All these kinds of information are set down on record. Decisions about what to put on record depend on the needs of the children and the predicted requirements of the people who will have access to the record. The school doctor does not necessarily need to know about how Russell and Julie are doing in their maths, but the teacher covering for you while you are away on a course would welcome that information. Each child and his or her parents should be privy to the widest range of information specifically about themselves, but not about other children. The headteacher may now require summary statements about the spread of performance within your class in relation to levels in National Curriculum attainment targets.

The kinds of things a teacher puts on record can be grouped like this:

- Administrative, including, for example, who is on roll, addresses and ages
- Teaching, including for example, what has been taught, lesson plans and evaluations
- Learning, including, for example, who has mastered specific concepts and can read given books
- Personal, including health problems, details of the home background, specific social skills and problems.

During the course of their work, classteachers need to keep all these kinds of record. The latter two are the kinds that concern us in this book, and they are related to individual children.

Records about individual children

Teachers should keep two kinds of record about children: records of the past and records of the future.

Academic: past Almost all that teachers write down about the children in their care relates to what has already happened. Typically, records have to do with children's achievements and problems. Thus for each child many teachers are keeping records of:

- Levels worked on in the attainment targets in foundation subjects
- Levels mastered in these attainment targets
- Written work and drawing (including samples taken periodically)
- Test results.

Personal and social: past In addition teachers often record some personal details:

- Social development and skills
- Home background and health problems
- Details of past referrals, for example sight, hearing, special needs.

The assembly of collections of records for a particular child, related to the past, can be seen as the construction of a *portfolio*. There is no requirement to go beyond ensuring the presence of the appropriate documents in a child's folder.

A sample portfolio

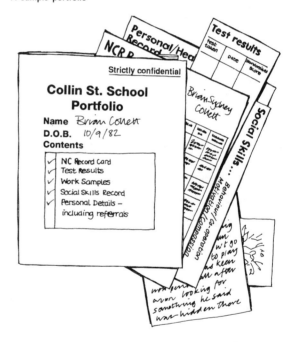

Academic: future In contrast, to focus on the child's future rather than the past, we need to record the following:

- Curriculum areas for potential growth, where the child has had past success
- Curriculum areas for remediation, where there is little progress.

Personal and social: future In addition, the following are helpful to children, their parents, teachers and other adults:

- Social development profile, including indications of areas for growth, increased responsibility and greater social skill
- Health problems affecting the future
- Special needs.

Records of the future contain many of the features of a *profile* in that they have a developmental relationship with records of the past and are an attempt to draw information together. This contrasts with the notion of the portfolio. Profiles are discussed in more detail below.

Here is a summary chart of possible child records.

Figure 5.1 Types of records of children's learning

	PORTFOLIO (ACHIEVEMENTS)
Records of the past	Levels reached Test results Work samples Teachers' comments
	PROFILE (POTENTIAL)
Records of the future	Next step for learning (plans and predictions) Areas of social development ready for extension Creative talents to be explored Teachers' predictive comments

Both of these kinds of records can be used to provide the information necessary to compile reports. There are a variety of ways in which records can be set out. We shall look at some of these possibilities next.

Compiling and presenting records and reports

The full range of kinds of report have precedents. We are all familiar with reports that are little more than a checklist. Here is one from the 1950s:

P

LONDON COUNTY COUNCIL

SCHOOL

REPORT FOR YEAR ENDING July 19 56

Name Hilary Dodson   Number in Class 45

Class 1   Position in Class 2

SUBJECT	ASSESSMENT	REMARKS
ENGLISH	Very good	
ARITHMETIC	Very good	
HISTORY	Good	
GEOGRAPHY		
SCIENCE Nature Study	Good	
ART	Good	
WRITING	Very good	
HANDWORK Needle work	Very good	
OTHER SUBJECTS Practical commonsense	Excellent	

RELIGIOUS KNOWLEDGE Good   Attendance Excellent

GENERAL REPORT
She has been a most satisfactory pupil – it has been a pleasure to work with her.
Congratulations

J. Tate Class Master   K.M.Winters Head Master

Class Mistress   Head Mistress

(P.2)4 3 2 1

Checklists of single words, marks and grades have often been embellished with remarks that give little indication about next steps or future development. From a school report of 1963:

Form Master's Report

Although his position in the form in low, most of his teachers seem satisfied that he is working well.

S. G. Bradford

His school career has been very successful, having reached the highest standard — std. VIII. He is punctual, honest, and industrious, and possesses a kind disposition. He is good-mannered, neat and clean in appearance, and is above the average in intelligence. He has held responsible positions during the last few years in school, and has been school captain since June this year.

There is common ground in the extract above and the one below, which is the 1990 entry in a profile which will carry on through the child's school career:

Head Master's Report

He appears to be working well but is barely keeping up with the form.

WH Griffin

Attitude to learning: enthusiastic, Conscientious.

Relationship with others: excellent

Progress over the last year: Excellent.
Progress has been made in all areas of the Curriculum. Jocelyn shows a consistently mature attitude to her work.

Profiles, too, despite their 'new' feel, were around before any of us embarked on our own education. The following is part of a 'profile' written in 1931:

Common devices for record compilation

The ways records about children are compiled dictate the extent of information passed on and therefore the range of decisions and actions the recipient can take. For example, if you compile a tick list about Lola's maths achievements, that will only give the next teacher some clues about how Lola is working. A fuller picture of achievement would be presented by a recent work sample and comments on how quickly new concepts are grasped, how diligently and carefully the work is done, and how numerate Lola seems to be.

Types of recording in common use include tick lists, the allocation of marks and scores, the keeping of written records, and the use of case studies. We shall look at each of these in turn.

Tick lists We are all familiar with tick lists. They are used to record such things as the completion of a page of the mathematics scheme, the fact that a reading book or comprehension exercise is finished, or nowadays they might be seen in relation to the 'ticking off' of levels within attainment targets. Tick lists are used because they are quick and can offer at a glance some notion of progression. However, they are extremely crude devices and can lead to spurious interpretations. A tick showing that Paul has done page 57 of his mathematics says absolutely nothing about Paul's understanding, or whether he can apply what he understands.

We believe that tick lists should only be used as records of children's 'contact' with work. It is important not to give the same work to Gloria again, because you have forgotten what she did last week! A tick against Gloria's name should ensure she is not given the same thing twice. Tick lists should not be used in isolation. They have to have fuller and more

National Curriculum Science tick list reproduced from Clemson, W., and Clemson, D., *Blueprints Science 7–11, Teacher's Resource Book* (In the tick list: a = introduced to, b = has difficulty/needs more work, c = understood)

RECORD SHEET 2: ATs 2–6, 9–16
Key Stage Two

Name: Mike Smith
Level: 3
Year/Class: J2

AT	Standard a	b	c	Comments
2	✓		✓	Makes good contributions to group work. Birdwatching is his hobby and he is a member of the local Young Ornithologists.
3	✓		✓	
4	✓	✓		
5	✓			
6	✓			
9	✓	✓	✓	See AT 16
10	✓	✓		Mike has grasped the principles of work in these areas. He needs more practice in doing experimental work.
11	✓	✓		
12	✓	✓		
13	✓			
14	✓			
15	✓			
16	✓	✓	✓	Mike's interest and knowledge is extensive. Now working at Level 4 in this AT and AT9.

sophisticated records placed alongside them. Some teachers have attempted to extend the usefulness of the tick list by having systems of differentiated 'ticks'; dots and ticks, colour coding, part hatched boxes, and the construction of triangles a side at a time are examples of these extensions. Extending a tick list does enhance its usefulness, though it will still have the strengths of simplicity and speed, and at the same time the weaknesses of over-brevity and over-simplification.

When you construct a tick list, whether for your own use or for use across the school, check that as far as possible you have addressed the following problems:

- Is the layout clear for everyone using and interpreting it?

- Does a tick against an item mean exactly what you intended?
- Is there space to write, in addition to ticking, if necessary?
- Does the tick list fit in with the range of record-keeping devices in use? Testing this out may mean tracing where the tick list fits in the teaching to reporting process. (See Figure 5.2 below.)

Marks and scores Marks out of 10 and the assignment of reading ages are common within our system and have a long history of usage. They are seen by many parents as indicators of achievement because parents were themselves subject to the allocation of marks and scores. However, as we indicated in Chapter 3, the use of marks and scores is fraught with dangers, both in use and in interpretation.

Most primary teachers only use marks in limited ways. Common examples are spelling tests, mental arithmetic and tables tests, and formal comprehension exercises.

There is widespread use of standardised scores by primary teachers, derived from reading tests, verbal and non-verbal reasoning tests, 'bought-in' subject tests, etc.

Whilst the use of standardised scores is of some value, we are not so convinced of the value of the 'marks out of 10' approach. In

either case, the allocation of a number to a child can lead to spurious judgements and stereotyping. A child who gets 9/10 for spelling one week, and 4/10 the next has not suddenly forgotten how to spell! It may be important to know, say, Lucy's reading age, but it is also vital to have records of Lucy's reading experiences, attitudes to reading and study skills. These written records must be given status that at least equals that of the score. What Lucy's teacher puts 'on record' (and this includes what she says to Lucy about her reading, as well as what she writes down) has much more effect in helping Lucy next week and next term, than the results of any test. Marks and scores tend to have high status whilst being clearly reductionist.

If you bear in mind the considerable short-comings of marks and scores, and you still plan to assign them, it may be worth checking your plans against the following questions:

- Why do I need these marks or scores?
- Is a mark or score the only or the best way to record this achievement?
- What are the effects of giving marks/ scores? You may have to give some because of school, LEA or national directives, but for those you have control of, you should look at the effects on children, parents and colleagues.
- Am I undermining my own expertise by over-valuing marks and scores?

Figure 5.2

Written records   The form of written records depends on their main purposes. Notes on children are kept by teachers to assist their memories when planning future teaching, and also as a bank of information from which to retrieve entries for reports. It is also possible to write summaries during the process of a period of learning. Ways of compiling written commentaries and records are indicated in Chapter 4. The advantages of a written record are that it does demonstrate the teacher's insights and it allows for a fuller portrait to be drawn than is possible through tick lists, marks, grades or scores. Their biggest disadvantage is that they are time-consuming.

Because this form of record keeping takes up a lot of teacher time, it is worth analysing what you write down against what you feel would make an 'ideal' record, to see whether some of what you are currently doing is a waste of time.

Case-studies   Records for individual children are sometimes built up through the assembly of a record based upon a variety of perspectives, often including the views of a number of people. A case-study record could arise through:

- A case conference on a child at risk
- Classroom observation involving another teacher or student teacher
- The planned compilation by a teacher of a set of items focusing on individual children, or an area of curriculum or organisation.

The characteristics of case-studies are that they:

- Involve the use of observation
- Treat the child as a whole person and are therefore closer to an 'ideal' of assessment
- Support immediate practical outcomes.

There is a discussion of the use of observation in Chapter 4. The disadvantage of a case-study approach is that it often involves a great deal of time and is therefore impractical as an approach to record-keeping for large numbers of children.

You will, of course, use this kind of approach to set up referrals for children deemed to have special needs and to be at risk. It may also be appropriate to consider using a case-study approach for:

- Children with whom you have a personality clash
- Children whom you know little about, and who are often overlooked
- Problem areas of the curriculum
- Across curriculum learning (for example, health education).

Presenting reports

The words 'school report' seem to make most people over the age of about six grimace! We all (and this includes teachers) immediately think of reports to parents about ourselves, about our own children, and about the children we teach. The very idea of reports can make us fearful and apprehensive. Though teachers do sometimes send reports to their colleagues and to other professionals, these often contain categories of information which have been specifically requested, and the contents are 'impersonal'. Reports to parents differ from this, for they are not only important to the children and parents themselves, but are a powerful vehicle for teachers to demonstrate their expertise to a wide audience. They can, therefore, present problems to teachers.

Reports to parents have been a common feature of schooling for many years, and have probably always been viewed as extremely important by parents themselves. They have taken two forms: (a) consultations between classteachers and parents and (b) written reports and profiles.

MATHEMATICS Julie works quickly and confidently. She enjoys practical tasks and records clearly and logically.

LANGUAGE All aspects of language work are developing well. In order to gain meaning and great pleasure from interaction with text, Julie employs a wide range of reading skills. She writes with enthusiasm and imagination, declaims with great confidence and listens attentively. She is able both to follow and to give quite detailed and accurate instructions.

SCIENCE Julie shows great interest in all aspects of science. She works thoughtfully and imaginatively, showing precision in recorded information.

ART Julie is developing a wide range of ideas and skills. Her excellent observational work shows attention to fine detail – an aspect of Julie's ability which is reflected throughout the curriculum.

MUSIC Julie is able to repeat the most difficult rhythms. She listens effectively and describes music appropriately, with imagination and interest.

DANCE/DRAMA Julie strives to excel consistently. She often organises the group.

PHYSICAL EDUCATION Julie works well individually and in small groups. She enjoys a physical challenge.

HANDWRITING Julie is developing a clear and legible style, with pleasing individuality.

Written reports to parents Parents set great store by marks and comments sent to them by teachers. To honour the trust parents place in what you write, reports must be completed accurately. Even if you feel that it demeans children's achievements to cram them onto one sheet of paper, you are now required to furnish parents with information about their child in relation to the subjects within the National Curriculum at the very least. You must let parents know about their children's performance annually. There is some flexibility about reports made during key stages. Those made at the ends of key stages must include quite specific entries. Draft proposals for these are set out in Chapter 1.

Oral reports to parents Teachers can be nervous about talking to parents, because parents can be tense and defensive, and teachers may feel they could face criticism. Parents can be nervous about talking to teachers because teachers can be tense and defensive and because parents may feel that their child, and thereby their parenting, may be criticised.

From our own experience as teachers we feel that there is some mutual mistrust between teachers and parents regarding the powers of judgement each has. There are two important areas of development where teachers have insights that parents do not. These are in stating the following:

- How a child is coping in an institutional setting which is different from and independent of home

- How a child's progress is evident in work done for those curriculum areas where the child's parents have little expertise or knowledge of how children learn.

Additionally, teachers can sometimes say:

- How a child's work compares with that of others of the same age, through norm-referenced testing (if this is appropriate).

Teachers must recognise that parents have experience of, and may possibly have insight into all other aspects of the development of their child, no matter how difficult they find it to express their perceptions. Teachers and parents are partners in a common enterprise: that is to allow, enable and promote children's intellectual development to its optimum. With this in mind, teachers as sensitive professional people can approach the annual parents' evenings with the following things in mind:

- The consultation should further co-operation rather than confrontation

- There are usually as many positive things that you can say about a child as there are problems

- Time for consultation is often short, so do make sure that you say all the important things that you intended (otherwise there is a danger of lying by omission)

- If you meet with parents who are intransigent and hostile, ask them politely if they will please discuss the matter further with the headteacher, who should be on hand

- The next day consult with your head-teacher to see if you can begin to engage the parents mentioned above in ways that will help you and them to help their child.

Reports to other teachers Reports to other teachers as children progress in a school or move to another school are commonly achieved through the compilation of written records and standardised scores. Within a school there is also an important element of oral reporting. This is less common, or significant, between schools.

In your reporting to other teachers, whether orally or in writing, you need to be aware of the following:

- There is a mutual trust between you and your colleagues which affects the content and delivery of the reports

  For example, nobody should hear from a third party about how teacher Mrs Barty has something against the four Higgins children, or about teacher Miss Gowan's spelling. If you have *anything* to say about a report passed to you internally, talk to the person who wrote it.

- Parents and children have trust in your professional discretion

  Be discreet in your oral reporting; for example, do not be tempted to discuss Willy's latest misdemeanor in front of 'helper mums'.

Using standard report forms Most teachers have two sorts of standard report forms to complete. There are school reports, the format of which is decided internally, and reports which are required by local authorities and which will follow children through their schooling. Whilst it is not possible to appraise these in detail due to their current diversity, they do share some common characteristics which are worth noting and reflecting upon.

We may feel, when faced with printed forms, that there is a mismatch between what we want to say and the expectations built into the form; there are always boxes which it is not easy to tick without a comment; there is often not enough room for written comments, and there are areas which are left out which we feel to be important. These feelings are partly due to the fact that we are now used to, and have raised expectations about, full and comprehensive information across our daily lives.

A printed report form meets your needs as a reporter if:

- It is easy to understand
- There is sufficient space for entries
- The categories of information asked for are all relevant
- There are no important omissions.

If you are asked to complete printed reports which are gravely at fault in any of the above respects, it is for you to try to get the form modified. Remember that other teachers may be willing to go on trying with forms that are unclear and unworkable. If that is the case, it is the children who will ultimately suffer.

Developments in records and reports

As we stated early in this book we believe that there will be major changes in the style and scope of records and reports in the future. Whilst the introduction of the National Curriculum and associated assessment is a major factor in these changes, it is clear that there are other important influences. Notable amongst these is the field of vocational education and the requirement for there to be documentation which reflects individual capabilities and achievements. The *profiling* of individuals grew in momentum in the 1980s and, we believe, will be seen to be a part of the work of all primary teachers in the 1990s.

The production of profiles for individual children has two major consequences. Firstly, there is a blurring of the common distinctions made between records and reports, and secondly there is a need to provide broad, coherent records rather than sets of marks. It is possible to divorce the accumulation of data from the reports produced after analysis of that data, but this is more difficult within a profiling system. Profiling makes demands of all the people taking part, as far as negotiation and exchange of information are concerned. It therefore makes sense to match what emerges in a profile with what goes on during the whole course of its compilation.

However, it is important here to make it absolutely clear that profiling is not a form of assessment. It is a coherent system of record-keeping and associated reporting. The outcomes of any assessments will constitute one form of record for the profile. Other records will be necessary. These range from teachers' written comments to what children say about their work. Indeed, some systems of profiling embrace children's own contributions about personal achievements, both within and outside school. In these, children have both the right and the responsibility to make entries in their profile. These achievements can include things such as getting a badge at Brownies, taking part in a village fête, or having a painting on display in the local library.

With a form of recording and reporting which is all-embracing, the problem is in assembling the data without leaving anything out. While profiles need to be open-ended, in the sense that they allow a different range of entries for each individual child, they also need structure to ensure there are no major omissions. Overleaf is a sample profile, showing a few of the kinds of categories of information which may be included.

Figure 5.3 A sample profile, taken from Dean, J. *Organising Learning in the Primary Classroom*, Croom Helm, 1983

	++	+	av	−	− −	
Imaginative		×				Lacks imagination
Persevering				×		Gives up easily
Well organised			×			Disorganised
Confident	×					Lacks confidence
Persistent					×	Distractible
Cooperative				×		Uncooperative

Meeting the requirements of the law

Recording

Content   Despite the promise that:

> **"***The actual conduct and delivery of assessments and the determination of outcomes is for primary schools.***"**
> Draft. *The Education Reform Act 1988:* National Curriculum: Order under Section 4 for Assessment Arrangements in English, Mathematics and Science at key stage 1 para. 32.c

it is probable that whatever age-group you are teaching, you are going to be asked to complete some internal records which use the National Curriculum attainment targets as a backbone.

Presentation   It seems that teachers and headteachers have some flexibility about how they may compile children's records. Thus we read:

> **"***Teachers should maintain a record of each pupil's attainments for each attainment target. The Order does not, however, prescribe the form of such records. There is, for example, no statutory requirement that teachers should observe and keep records of each pupil's attainment against every statement of attainment throughout the key stage.***"**
> ibid. para. 16

On the face of it, this should fill teachers with cheer. At least they will be able to devise 'along-the-way' records themselves. The irony is that official statements to this effect may result in the emphasis being placed on National Curriculum summative records at the ends of key stages.

Reporting

To parents: content and presentation   Written reports sent home to parents will now become universal. DES Regulations (Records of Achievement, Circular 8/90) require

> ...**"***A written report on each pupil's achievements to reach his parents by 31 July in each year...***"**

The content of interim reports within key stages has not been specifically prescribed. Prescriptions at key stages will be detailed. The draft reporting requirements for core subjects at the end of key stage 1 (starting in 1991) are that reports should include, for each core subject, the level of attainment in:

- The subject as a whole
- Each profile component
- Each attainment target (this record may be supplied to parents on request, or, without request, at the school's discretion).

There will be similar requirements regarding the other foundation subjects in due course. There are no national prescriptions regarding reporting format, but in *The Education (Individual Pupils' Achievements) (Information) Regulations 1990* (DES) there is a suggested basic format for the end of key stage 1, 1991, which is reproduced overleaf. Entries on this suggested form may need changing in the light of reductions in statutory assessment requirements.

The National Curriculum Council has made recommendations about the above DES Regulations. Some of their suggestions are listed at the bottom of this page.

We would support moves to make reports reflect all that children do in school, but favour forms which allow teachers to make full comments, rather than the insistence that they use devices such as graphs to represent achievement. Our misgivings about summary records are that they are reductionist.

To the community Headteachers are not required to publish statistics in their annual reports or prospectuses showing how many children reached which levels of the National Curriculum at the end of key stage 1. The Secretary of State will, however, encourage primary schools to do so from 1992 onwards. Aggregate results at key stage 2 must be published by law from 1995.

Nationally Schools will be expected to send in statistical information for monitoring, evaluation and national statistical purposes.

There is a danger that, with published school statistics and local financial management, the National Curriculum and its assessment could be used to fundamentally affect the status and accountability of teachers. If a school's published results are good, will not more parents choose that school for their children, and will not that school then acquire better staffing ratios, more funding, more of everything? Compare a school in this situation with one in an area of social deprivation which may, despite all the teachers' efforts, experience none of these advantages. This looks very much like 'payment by results'. Fortunately there are some possible ways of offsetting invidious comparisons between schools. These include, for example, federating with other local schools, engaging parents in their children's education in ways that are not exclusively concerned with published results, and enlisting the help of Higher Education institutions as allies in resourcing.

- The regulations should require the reporting of progress in the whole curriculum
- Progress in the foundation subjects should be reported at AT level and in narrative
- There should be a mandatory form with a graphical description of achievement in each AT and room for a descriptive account of the pupil's progress and attainment in each subject
- Schools should be required to use the same system of reporting every year
- The circular should make clear that reporting can take place at any time during the year
- The regulations should require the implementation of a summary record of achievement.

NCC suggestions from page 13 NCC News, Issue No 3, April 1990.

Figure 5.4 Record format suggested by the DES, 1990

REPORT ON PUPIL ACHIEVEMENT

ANNEX B
SCHOOL YEAR . . . .

Pupil . . . . School . . . . LEA (where applicable) . . . .

Signature of Headteacher . . . . Date . . . .

NATIONAL CURRICULUM

1. ACHIEVEMENTS IN SUBJECTS STATUTORILY ASSESSED (END OF KEY STAGE . . .)*

	Achievement in Profile Component	Achievement in subject overall
English	Speaking and listening	
	Reading	
	Writing	
Mathematics	Number, algebra and measures	
	Shape, space, data handling	
Science	Exploration	
	Knowledge/understanding	

2. ACHIEVEMENTS IN SUBJECTS NOT STATUTORILY ASSESSED

Technology	
History	
Geography	
Art	
Music	
Physical Education	

*The numbered levels of achievement set out here represent summaries of more detailed information which the school will let you have if given notice that you want it. Where a pupil has been exempted from any of the relevant requirements, details are set out on an accompanying sheet.

82

Records in action: Data collection to finished record

If we spell out the steps to be followed in producing an assessment record suitable for your colleagues to see, the process can be set out diagrammatically as shown below in Figure 5.5.

As you can see, there are three essential steps. You may be able to compile records without writing down all three stages, but you will need to go through these steps nevertheless. There follows an example worked through from the point at which the child does some work to the progress entry on the school internal record.

Everyday classroom records: an example

The first stage in producing a record is classroom data collection. In Chapter 4 we indicated some ways of collecting information about children, and gave some suggestions as to how you may set out the information. In thinking about the next steps in record construction we found it helpful to go back to the initial pool of information on which

teachers draw to make their assessments. In Chapter 4 we defined the 'pool' as comprising the following things that children do: oral/aural, reading, practical, written, research, co-ordination and control and aesthetic. We then looked carefully at the examples which we attached to each of these labels, in order to devise succinct ways of making a record of them. On inspection, all the 'things children do' can readily be divided into two sub-groups. The first of these comprises 'acts which move work along'. Though they require thinking and decision-making, they are not content bound. We have called these *skills*. The remaining acts, which require substantive content, we have labelled *applications*. We have listed some examples of skills and applications for each of the kinds of things children do in school in Figure 5.6 overleaf.

Using the groupings in Figure 5.6, all that a child has done can be entered on an 'array chart' like the one in Figure 5.7 on page 85.

Decisions about what to put in records that other teachers will want to see can be made on the basis of information displayed in an array chart. Some of these details might readily transfer onto school achievement records that

Figure 5.5 Processes in record creation

PRE REQUISITES FOR RECORD CREATION		STEPS IN RECORD CREATION		
		1. ABRIDGEMENT	2. INTERPRETATION	3. TRANSLATION
CHILD ACTION	TEACHER COLLECTION	Teacher writes down a résumé	Teacher converts information into child record	Teacher ties child record to National Curriculum attainment targets
Speaks	Observes			
Listens	Listens			
Reads	Participates			
Does practical work	Scrutinises written work	Teacher summarises outcomes		
Writes	Tests	Teacher works out scores		
Researches				
Moves and controls				

Figure 5.6 Skills and applications

WHAT CHILDREN DO IN SCHOOL	EXAMPLES OF SKILLS	EXAMPLES OF APPLICATIONS
Oral/aural	Oral: Articulation Vocabulary Grammar Aural: Articulation Listening	Answering questions 'Sharing time' Talking about events Describing activities Responding to stimuli (TV, pictures, artefacts) Reading aloud Presentation in assembly
Reading	Memory Word-building Anticipation Recall	Aloud and 'silently' Stories Poems Information
Practical	Assembling equipment Observation Use of other senses	Setting up experiments Making things happen Controlling variables Collecting results Modifying the outcomes
Written	Letter shapes and conventions Use of computer keyboard Spelling Punctuation	'Answers' Lists, poems, feelings, thoughts Imaginative stories Reports of real events
Research	Elements of skills in all other categories including those for: Communication Study Access	Analysis (for example, working out the questions to ask, problems to solve, and accessing information) Synthesis (for example, sifting and collating information for reporting)
Co-ordination and control	Handling pencils, pens, chalks, brushes, scissors Throwing, catching, hitting and kicking a ball Gymnastics and body awareness	Writing, drawing, painting and model-making Playing ball games Dance and gymnastic routines

are tied closely to the detailed prescription of the attainment targets in core and other foundation subjects. For example, in an array chart oral/aural section the entries may contain:

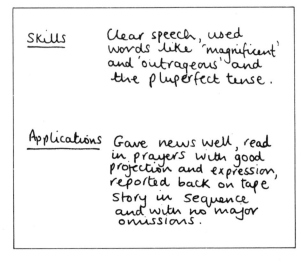

These items all contribute to English AT1 Speaking and listening.

Records and professional integrity

Records of children's learning can affect irrevocable decisions about their futures. It is imperative, therefore, that teachers do their utmost to see that records do not misrepresent children. There are a number of ways in which this can happen. There follows a discussion of some examples.

Lying by omission

In their anxiety about wrongly 'labelling' children teachers sometimes leave out of records things that should really be there. It may be that the behavioural problems that Dominic has shown over the year in your class will disappear when he is in the care of a teacher with a different approach. On the

Figure 5.7 Child-week array chart

NAME: **DATE:**

	ORAL/AURAL	READING	PRACTICAL	WRITING	RESEARCH	CO-ORDINATION
S K I L L S						
A P P L I C A T I O N S						
N C ATs SUBJECTS						

other hand they may not, and strategies that you have tried with Dominic will be helpful to the next teacher in deciding what approach he or she should try.

Speculation

Teachers are experienced in developing rationales for children's progress, or lack of it. These are often based on only partial information of, for example, what the child's past and present home life is like, and on the teacher's own experience of children, whether his or her own or others. Every child is unique, and comparisons between the life experiences, personalities and resultant performances of children are invidious. There are considerable risks in setting down your suppositions about children, unless you can substantiate them.

Choosing your words

In old-style reports teachers used 'Very fair' to mean less good than 'Fair', when 'Fair' meant 'Fairly good'! As far as possible, we suggest you try to avoid any unusual, idiosyncratic or even over-use of particular words. Remember, the intention is to communicate without misrepresentation or misunderstanding.

Confidentiality and security

Records should only be accessible to specified people. This may include your colleagues, the headteacher and other professional agencies to whom children are referred. You should be aware of the regulations regarding parental access to their own children's records. When you have had sight of a record you need to keep its contents confidential. You are betraying a trust if you disclose what is on record to people who should not have access to it, and that includes disclosure by word of mouth. Records also need to be kept safe, for they are often irreplaceable.

Understanding and action   Be sure that you read, understand and act on records that come to you. The whole record-keeping process is rendered meaningless if teachers fail to act on it.

Summary

Record-keeping and reporting have for decades been seen by many people as part of a teacher's job. Now teachers face additional pressures of legislation which affect record-keeping and reporting content, presentation and procedures. Despite the influence of parents (who may see formal reports as a cornerstone of schooling) and the compulsion to look at levels, marks, scores and weightings, and do seemingly meaningless things with them, we hope that teachers will not lose sight of the main function of the records they keep.

Teachers are there to prepare our children for tomorrow. They do this not only through providing imaginative teaching and learning opportunities, but also through implementing creative record-keeping and reporting strategies. Records and reports profoundly affect the decisions made about children by their parents, their teachers and their employers. Even more importantly they have irrevocable effects on children themselves. They may lead children to follow courses, take exams and look for jobs that fit the record rather than their dreams. They sometimes also press children to underestimate their worth and their potential. In our records and reports we need to accommodate the demands of parents, employers and the law, while having as our focus the needs of children. A 'good' record is clear, succinct and apposite. It is also one that inspires every person who sees it, including the child him or herself, to invest in the future development of the whole human being whose name appears at the top.

6

MANAGING ASSESSMENT: THE IMPLICATIONS FOR SCHOOLS AND TEACHERS

No matter how committed you are to the importance of assessment, and no matter how expert you are in ways of doing it and knowing the technical terms to use, it will be all to no avail if you cannot be a good manager.

However, there are many problems involved in the organisation and management of assessment, some of which can be difficult to solve. It is these that feature high on the list of issues taken up by the teaching unions. Being an assessment organiser and manager does place great demands on teachers. You need to be really creative and flexible to do assessment well, while at the same time teaching well.

Throughout this book we have stressed that, in order to be valid and useful, assessment must be seen as an integral part of the whole pattern of activity in school. Discussion of the organisation and management of assessment should not be confined to such things as the organisation of a test, or the management of a SAT. We need to consider the major elements involved in making learning opportunities. This chapter, therefore, contains material which could be applied to a whole range of management issues in school. What we have done here is to address these in respect of assessment.

It is not possible, or even desirable, for us to offer detailed prescriptions for the implementation of organisation and management structures and systems within a school; each school is a unique community with its own traditions, mores and priorities. Instead, in this chapter we aim to identify what we see as the most important general items for discussion and resolution in all primary schools and classrooms.

We have split the chapter into two parts, in order to discuss the issues at school and class level. The areas for consideration at both levels are the same; they differ in terms of their emphasis, scope and range of effects. The major area, and the one which underpins all of the others is *planning*. The priority areas within the planning which is necessary for the management of assessment are:

- Staff and children
- Curriculum
- Time
- Change.

School assessment plans

The planning process

Ordered planning is fundamental to good practice in schools. This indication has come strongly from HMI in the 1980s. It seems that many teachers have not actually given planning a particularly high priority. For some, this reflects a concern that predetermination of goals will remove the spontaneity and serendipity in learning and teaching. We too would not wish to see over-prescription of children's learning opportunities. Indeed, some of our reservations about the development of the National Curriculum are about its possible implementation as 'over-planned', narrow, content-based teaching. However, as a framework it does offer possibilities for flexibility and creativeness, but only with sophisticated planning. Planning needs to be seen as systematic whilst open to modification; it should not be seen as responding to outside, conformist views. Whilst common planning issues can be identified for all schools, it is important that teachers in a school grapple with these issues within the context of their particular institution's set of strengths and resources.

Planning periods   All planning should be for a specific fixed term. This may not have been the case for all management planning in the past. Schools do commonly plan such things as school concerts, sports and parents' meetings well in advance. There is typically at least a term's warning and preparation and there is often the experience of previous years to help guide these events. It has not been the rule in all schools that things such as staff development possibilities and class plans have been put in the context of whole-school management planning. Schools are now, though, going to have to plan for more than traditional events. With the advent of local management and delegated budgets, and the new requirements of National Curriculum assessments, it is vital that schools look at planning in at least

three different time periods. As far as assessment is concerned they might be as follows:

- Short-term plans (about 3 months) should include reviews of data collection, day-to-day staff communications, reminders of important dates, and collective reviews of continuity and progression
- Medium-term plans (one year) should include feedback from three monthly (or termly) reviews, planned communications with parents and governors, annual calendar of events, collective reviews of progress, up-dating of long-term plans and reporting arrangements
- Long-term plans (three to five years) should include short- and medium-term plans in relation to key stages, and curriculum implementation and change. The long-term plan needs rewriting every year.

Setting up and delivering assessment plans
At the heart of initiating and carrying through the school assessment plans is the need to be certain that your plans are centred on the real issues. They should not be a set of responsive items brought forward through the pressures of the here and now. There are four assessment planning issues that we think all schools must address. These are to do with support for:

- Staff
- Curriculum delivery
- The effective use of time
- Innovation and change.

Support for staff

At the school level particular consideration must be given to the staff. Whilst we are engaged in an enterprise pre-eminently about children's learning, it is clear that the forging of a strong staff team with a positive commitment to the job is a priority at the school level.

Curriculum development is quintessentially about staff development. This assertion leads us to concentrate on staff roles and responsibilities, teamwork, and professional development.

Roles and responsibilities   Over recent years there has been an increased tendency for headteachers to refine and tighten up the descriptions of teaching jobs which carry increased levels of remuneration. Gone are the days of responsibility allowances for country dancing or keeping the stock cupboards tidy, if those days ever really existed. We are now faced with a set of hefty and complex responsibilities for all. Job descriptions for all staff, regardless of their special responsibilities, will have to be written in some detail; one item which will appear on all job descriptions will be to do with the role of the teacher in respect of assessment. We would suggest that, in developing your school plans, you agree teacher job descriptions which include items such as:

- Undertaking Teacher Assessments using a variety of assessment techniques
- Keeping up-to-date records in accordance with the school record system
- Providing information, in an appropriate form, as required by the headteacher
- Participation in the school's annual review of assessment procedures
- Contributing to key stage assessments.

Additionally, our experience would indicate that assessment co-ordination must be undertaken by a named person; it cannot be pursued as a collective. In some schools this co-ordination might be undertaken by the headteacher, in others there may be an assessment co-ordinator. The duties will include:

- Providing colleagues with information about national and local requirements

- Ensuring that any school systems are both understood and adhered to across the school
- Providing regular opportunities for evaluation, and ensuring that action is taken on the agreed outcomes of evaluation meetings
- Trouble-shooting
- Giving colleagues appropriate briefings prior to parents' and governors' meetings
- Developing moderation and cross-moderation opportunities.

As with curriculum development, the development of good assessment systems is inextricably linked with staff development. If a school is to establish a reputation for good practice, it is essential that the continuing professional development of all members of the staff team is given a high priority.

An example of part of a job description

```
- Provide      learning    oppor-
  tunities for R and Y1 children

- Undertake    TA    and    compile
  appropriate records

- Co-ordinate  work  of  other
  teachers of R and Y1 children

- Select and organise R and Y1
  resources

- Liaise with pre-school groups
  and parents

- Liaise        with        other
  co-ordinators

- Participate in annual reviews
  of school development plans
  and assessment procedures
```

Teamwork A 5–16 'all-through' National Curriculum with assessments at predetermined key stages has destroyed the notion of individual classteacher autonomy at a stroke. This loss of autonomy has caused many teachers the greatest anxiety in this period of radical change. However, we would question the idea that classteachers were ever self-governing and self-determining. It was always the case that a teacher had to see him or herself in the context of the 'seamless robe'; no single classteacher ever completely educated a child in one year, or even several years. We do recognise that many teachers have taken comfort in being able to close the classroom door and shut themselves off from the rest of the school. But this is not autonomy, it is insecurity! We are now at a point at which no one can be allowed to remove themselves from the community of the school and the management decisions made within it.

In organising and managing assessment all teachers in a school are now going to have to undertake a collaborative and co-operative approach to their work. In addition to the adoption of strategies for team teaching, the need for team assessment approaches. To assess the work of a specific group of children picked out from the whole class requires a co-operative teaching approach. This is also the case with regard to ensuring appropriate expertise in all areas of the curriculum, whether for teaching, learning or assessment.

Communications between schools will also have to become fuller and more frequent. Schools are charged with the responsibility of offering each child full and appropriate access to the National Curriculum according to their needs and achievements, across all levels and phases of education. This will only be accomplished through collaborative activity involving the entire staff, working together both within their own school, and with other schools with which they have links.

Staff development The recent developments in assessment, record-keeping and reporting mean that all teachers are going to become more expert assessors. Whilst all primary teachers have some experience of particular forms of assessment and the use of a range of tests and related devices, many are not familiar with assessment principles or the role of assessor. Schools are going to have to make plans which will ensure that, within the staff team, there is expertise in:

- Record-keeping
- Reporting
- Profiling
- Interpretation of assessment information
- Data collection techniques
- Organisation of assessment opportunities.

Support for curriculum delivery

We are using the word 'curriculum' to mean the planned set of activities and learning opportunities offered by a school. Associated with this planned offering is an assessment system. It is possible to find schools in which the modes of assessment do not match the custom and practice of that school in terms of its curriculum delivery. For example, recent concerns about reading standards have opened up a discussion about the appropriateness of the forms of assessment being used to establish reading achievement scores. To polarise this, the question might be whether a phonics based reading test offers a proper reflection of children's progress in a school which uses a real book approach.

Managing assessment must be seen as a joint, inextricably linked exercise in relation to the management of the school's curriculum. There are three major issues which appear on the curriculum and assessment agenda. These are:

- The ways in which the curriculum is offered
- The handling of across-curriculum issues

in the context of:

- The relationship of the whole curriculum in a particular school to the National Curriculum.

Modes of delivery The two central dimensions of delivery are the teaching approach and the nature of the content. To establish appropriate assessment systems it is necessary to firstly work out the desired, and actual, modes of curriculum delivery within and across the school. Note that the assessment mode adopted must match the desired delivery, and not the other way round!

There are a variety of ways in which the National Curriculum can be delivered. For example, it may be appropriate to adopt a straightforward 'linear' approach in some schools, where discrete subjects are taught level by level, as they appear in the Statutory Orders. In others, right across the school a 'modular' approach may be adopted, where ATs are grouped and taught together at points in the year. Yet other schools may go for a more 'mixed', maybe even thematic approach, straddling ATs within and across subjects. All these approaches call for different assessment plans. Some suggestions are set out in Figure 6.1.

Across-curriculum issues In addition to the foundation subjects defined in the National Curriculum there is a requirement that schools pay attention to other areas of learning, including:

- Health
- Gender
- Multicultural issues
- Economic awareness
- Political and international understanding
- Environmental education.

Of these, whilst all should be evaluated in school, we will concentrate on the implications of gender and culture. Assessments can be fraught with unintended bias in these areas. With regard to gender, for example, much research has been done which supports the idea that practical tests and multiple-choice format tests favour boys over girls. When looking at children's oral skills, we need to be sure to give all the children chances to speak out. Research supports the idea that in mixed groups, girls offer less of a contribution than boys. The key is, that just as in teaching and learning, we must do all in our power to offer all children equal opportunities in assessment. At a school level this does mean having an articulated policy about eliminating sexism and dealing with the evidence of it when it arises, whether it occurs in the classroom or in the playground, and whether it arises from teacher, children, resources or assessment procedures.

Figure 6.1 National Curriculum delivery and assessment

MODE OF NATIONAL CURRICULUM DELIVERY	MODES OF ASSESSMENT MANAGEMENT
Linear	TA frequent. All subject assessment carried forward simultaneously
Modular	TA modular, followed by consolidation/remediation/new module and then a new phase of TA
Mixed thematic	TA using both frequent and modular approaches

With regard to culture, the issues are again complex and need sensitive handling. The National Curriculum seems to have been planned to meet the needs of the majority of the indigenous population, without any special provision being made for other groups of young people. In fact a subject-labelled curriculum is bound to be culturally discrete. It makes a whole host of assumptions about, for example, how we think, how we learn and what is important in school; it also has an underlying and hidden rationale about, for example, what concepts mean and the nature of knowledge and scholarship. The importance of all this for assessment purposes is that there has to be a whole-school policy about equal opportunities, and vigilance for signs that the policy is not being reflected in the management or delivery of assessments across the school.

A possible extract from a school prospectus

The headteacher and staff of this school do all in their power, in their provision of learning opportunities and in the assessment of children's learning, to ensure that:
. . . 'each pupil . . . (has) . . . a broad and balanced curriculum which is also relevant to his or her particular needs . . .'
. . . 'the curriculum . . . (is) . . . fully taken up by each individual pupil.'
Each pupil develops . . . 'as an individual, as a member of society and as a future adult member of the community with a range of personal and social opportunities and responsibilities.'

(para 2.2. *National Curriculum: From Policy to Practice,* DES 1989)

The school and the National Curriculum

The organisational structures and the management systems within the school must support full engagement with the National Curriculum. In some cases this is going to mean quite radical changes from existing practice in terms of the balance of curriculum content, the timetabling of activities, the jobs undertaken by staff and the assessment arrangements of the school. Assessment changes, or suggested developments, must be constantly evaluated against the minimum requirements of the National Curriculum. The whole curriculum and its assessment is also an issue for school level decisions.

Support for the effective use of time

There is now sufficient evidence to support the assertion that the more time the children spend on task, the greater the likelihood of them achieving their potential. The first major consideration, then, has to do with the management of the contact time that children can have, and ensuring that this is at the optimum level. There are two facets to this optimisation; they are:

● The construction of a timetable
● The development of systems which ensure maximum uninterrupted time on each task.

Timetables Whilst schools will always differ with regard to starting and finishing times, lengths and numbers of playtimes and so on, the advent of the National Curriculum and associated assessment will mean that schools develop some very similar patterns of time allocations to subject areas. How this is done, and how schools handle the resulting status of certain subjects, will fundamentally affect how the school is perceived. School timetables must still offer a degree of flexibility so that chances for innovation and creative opportunism can be grasped. Individual class-teachers should still have a major influence within their own classrooms, providing that they support allocations of time agreed across the school. Flexible timetabling enhances the possibility for the use of thematic and topic-based work as well as necessary across-curriculum work. However, it will be essential for schools to have detailed timetabling of events and scarce resources in order for assessments to be sensibly and strategically programmed.

Time on task   One of the major strengths of the primary school is the sense of community and the power of the concomitant shared relationships. However, this is also the major Achilles' heel of many of our primary schools: in order to honour the principles of 'belonging' and 'participation', some headteachers and classteachers interrupt teaching and learning frequently and often inappropriately. Interruptions for money collections, unexpected visitors, telephone messages, and changes in the normal school-day pattern are inevitable; but all too often these devices are used in place of a better planned and organised communication system. Teachers should not be available to outsiders at the drop of a hat during their contact time with children, whether they are teaching or assessing. The children should be equally unavailable. Schools have to have systems of communication which do not impinge on teaching and learning and assessing time, but which rather take advantage of those times when colleagues are officially available.

Support for innovation and change

Assessment management needs constant review, updating and change. It can be difficult to instigate. Assessments that are exclusively about performance and ignore potential are obstacles to change in all respects. In order to ensure that you are not in an assessment rut, it is essential that there is at least one staff meeting a year in which there is a thorough feedback on the whole range of assessments and record-keeping approaches and management of these within the school. This meeting must offer 'feedforward' as well as feedback. In establishing a system where possibilities for change are built in, there are two themes which run across and through all the sections in this chapter: communications and evaluation.

Communications   In the development of school plans it is essential that the plans become 'owned' by the staff team. For this to happen it is necessary to engage everyone in the preparation of the plans and for all staff to commit themselves to achieving the purposes of the plans. This process is rooted in open, regular and sincere communication. This communication must be multi-way. The pay-off in assessment terms is threefold:

- The likelihood of informative recording in school is considerably enhanced
- Communications with parents are likely to be both positive and formative
- Staff morale, involvement and motivation are enhanced.

Evaluation   By 'evaluation' we are referring to the set of professional activities whereby teachers regularly and systematically appraise themselves in relation to the development of the children and the proffered set of learning opportunities. It is vital that evaluations are not based exclusively on assessment information. It is inappropriate to restrict the valuing of the work of the school to 'results'. The examination of the subtle interplay of teaching approaches, relationships and growth in personal and professional knowledge and skills needs more data than can be provided by assessment of the children's work. It is important, though, that the school ensures that the assessment systems in operation can be linked into the wider evaluation.

TEN 'MUSTS' FOR SCHOOL ASSESSMENT MANAGEMENT

1 Assessment arrangements must be planned
2 Staff teams must work and plan together
3 Assessment must be co-ordinated across the school
4 Staff development for assessment must be made available
5 The school curriculum must embrace across-curriculum issues as well as subjects
6 The school curriculum must embrace the National Curriculum
7 There must be a school assessment calendar
8 Children and staff must be given sufficient time on task
9 Assessment arrangements must be developed in the light of evaluative information supported by effective communication
10 Whole-school plans need working through in all classes in the school.

Class assessment plans

The importance of planning

Good planning is essential for teaching, learning and assessment. You are a manager and monitor of teaching and learning. You would not expect managers in any other job to start a day's work without a plan which covered not only what will happen that day, but months and even years ahead. You would also expect a manager in any other field to know the strongest and weakest parts of his or her operation. So too in teaching you need to have plans of various kinds, and you will be able to see where things are working excellently or not going so well by doing evaluation and assessment. What we have said in relation to whole-school planning can be mirrored in the classroom. Planning needs to cater for different time horizons, to support a coherent set of learning opportunities for the children, and to enhance both continuity and progression.

Planning periods As with whole-school planning there are three time spans to consider. The progress of the children over the year is the long-term element, with each school term being the medium-term building block. The formal periods for assessing and report preparation must be identified and put on the school calendar. Much of the assessment work will be teacher assessment and this needs to be planned in detail over the short periods. For example, a short-term planning period might go like this:

> Plan in detail what you wish to achieve over a period of time, say four weeks. Write a timetable for yourself for that period. Plan what the children in your class should achieve during that time. Write a timetable for them; then plan a week, down to the details of each session, firstly for yourself and then for the children. Mark in possible assessment points on the timetable. Carry it through for a week. Collate and evaluate teaching, learning and assessment. Modify the next week's plan accordingly. Start to project what the next four-week period plan may comprise.

Setting up and delivering assessment plans
Classteachers need to establish the levels of achievement for each individual early in the school year. This may be done, unless you are a reception teacher, through the interrogation

of existing reports and, where necessary, past-performance related activities set by you early in the term. At the end of the first month you should have a set of profiles about each child which will permit you to ensure their continued progression. Such profiles should be amenable to additions over the year, thereby easing the pressures of reporting at the end of the year.

Having established base-line starting points, it is then essential that there is a plan for the delivery of new material together with consolidation and remediation activities. It is likely that such planning will have to be based upon the use of groups as the basic unit of planning rather than the whole class or individuals. How you decide to deliver the curriculum will depend on school plans and your own predilections; your assessment should tie in with this. Some possibilities are spelled out in Figure 6.1 (see page 91).

Planning is the major issue for classteachers, as it is for the school as a whole. Class plans should always support:

● The people (in this case the children)
● The curriculum
● The effective use of time
● Change.

Support for children

Whilst there will be comparisons made between groups and across and between schools in terms of global National Curriculum results, we believe that the effectiveness and appropriateness of the National Curriculum, in humanitarian terms, will have to be evaluated through the outcome for individuals. Your planning, then, must have the individual child's progression as the major purpose. Some of the data for making assessments will come from children working alone and some must come from activity within a group setting. In addition to these assessments there will be some whole-class reporting. A priority,

then, in managing assessment in contact time is going to be the organisation of the class so that you have the opportunity to make assessments of individuals working alone and in group settings.

Individuals versus the group or class   Research has produced evidence which seems to indicate that the organisation and management of classrooms around individualised programmes is difficult to sustain and has some major disadvantages. Individual children seem to make the best progress in classrooms using group work combined with stimulating class lessons as a means of starting new work or consolidating what has been done. The value of the class lesson will, we believe, increasingly be seen as a stimulus for the thematic work of the class in general terms, and as a reminder to children of the central issues of work that have been covered. Additionally the whole-class situation can be used to reinforce the across-curriculum issues that children need to encounter and which run across all of the work that they do. This is discussed further under **Support for curriculum delivery** (see page 96). Planning should centre on ways of ensuring varied group activity, within which there is high quality individual learning.

Groupings for assessment   A common way of grouping children has been according to ability. Whilst a strong case can be made for ability grouping, especially in relation to English, the National Curriculum assessment requirements do mean that other forms of grouping should also be utilised. In planning work it will be important to look at strategies for grouping which permit maximum learning. Similarly, in grouping for assessment, we should try to permit children to do their best. You do need to consider groupings based upon, for example:

● Single sex (some girls and boys may perform better in this kind of grouping)

- A range of skills (useful in problem-solving and assessment of co-operative effort)
- Mixed reactions to test situations (less anxious children may help others to relax)
- Mixed adeptness at practical work (chances for peer group learning).

Children as managers   In undertaking group work and assessment it is necessary to ensure that the rest of the class is gainfully employed and not likely to disrupt the work on which the teacher wishes to concentrate at that moment. There are no ready solutions to issues of control. Certainly it is likely that disruption will be at a minimum when children are:

- Interested in the task/s
- Well 'matched' to the task in terms of current capability
- Able to tackle the work without constant support
- Capable of resourcing themselves appropriately
- Used to working in a group setting.

All of this would suggest that, in the early part of their school lives and then throughout it, children should be helped to view learning as something they do, not as something done to them. The reception class teacher has a key role in preparing children for the years of independent learning ahead, both at school and beyond. There are quite specific things that very young children can do, which come under the category of study skills. They include skills such as:

- Knowing where to find things they need for their work
- Being able to fetch and put together what they need for a job

- Being able to work amongst other people
- Knowing when their work is finished
- Knowing when their work is their best
- Being able to care for equipment
- Being able to tidy up.

Support for curriculum delivery

The issues for classteachers to consider are: how to deliver the National Curriculum and the whole curriculum; how across-curriculum work is realised; how the classwork relates to the whole-school plan.

Modes of delivery   In planning the delivery of the curriculum in the classroom, the central matters to be resolved are the following:

- What approach will you adopt to teaching and assessing National Curriculum?
- What other assessment requirements are built in to the whole curriculum?
- What are the specific assessment requirements of the children within this class?
- How do your assessment plans fit into the plans for the whole school?

The answers to these questions are unique to each classteacher and will change from year to year.

Across-curriculum and whole curriculum
Following from the discussions and decisions at the whole-school level there will be policies on such issues as gender and cultural diversity that you will need to subscribe to. For the children, you embody the ethos set by the staff of the school. Whatever the programme of activities you develop, it is most important that all the children in your care are allowed equal access, equal opportunity and optimal and equal assessment provision. This may include parts of the curriculum which you hate, have no expertise in, or believe they should not be doing. If it is the case that you

find it difficult to subscribe to aspects of the curriculum that you are required to offer, it must be in the context of the staff team, not the classroom, that your concerns are expressed. We may all know of the teacher who prefaces new work with 'This is boring but we have to do it . . .' and we are all aware of the effects of such an approach. These effects are often most noticeable in the outcomes of assessment!

Support for the effective use of time

Classteachers are very worried about how to fit National Curriculum assessment into their working lives. It may be that part of their worry is that there is no necessary link between externally constructed and validated tests and the day-to-day activities in their classrooms. We are entirely sympathetic with aspects of that view. However, the National Curriculum assessment arrangements do provide an opportunity to establish formative assessment at the heart of teaching and learning. In order to grasp the opportunity offered, it is necessary to rethink the use of time: both teacher time and pupil time.

Teacher time Teacher time is about organisation of contact with chosen individual children and groups of children. It is not the same as pupil time spent on task. In order to clearly distinguish between teacher and pupil time, it is necessary for you to consider the way in which your time is spent and to draw up a teacher timetable. At certain points in the week, such as when you are giving a whole-class lesson, your teacher timetable will coincide exactly with the pupil timetable; but for most of the time it will not. You need to establish your own agenda and work out how this will be accounted for in terms of time. While you are, for example, observing a group of children engaged in a practical activity, you will have set up the remaining children with tasks that they can carry through independently of you.

Pupil time Pupil time is about the time that children spend on task. It is also about the distribution of experiences over, say, a week or a day. Teachers control this time allocation but it is not the same as teaching time. It is better named as learning time. In order to maximise the use of available time it is vital that the classteacher, in agreement with other colleagues, helps to formulate school plans for timetabling and the guarding of time on task. Once formulated then everyone must play the game and stick to the agreed rules.

Support for innovation and change

As with the management of assessment across the school, it is essential that class arrangements are open to change and development. In other words we have to be responsive to the milieu of the classroom each year, and each year is different. There is a limit to the range of possible assessment techniques and approaches, but it is necessary to constantly evaluate your use of these and to be prepared to follow learning rather than see assessment as the leader to learning. 'I always give a test on Friday afternoons' has no place in good assessment practice; the information from a rigid assessment structure is unlikely to advance whole-school developments. Indeed, as with whole-school arrangements it is necessary to keep reviewing both communications and evaluation regarding assessment.

Communications What you do and find out in your classroom needs to be communicated in two ways. It must support the passing on of good, reliable and fair assessments of children to other teachers and it must inform the future development of assessment within your school and your own classroom.

Evaluation In order for you to review and update your assessment plans you need to match them against the quality of the assessment information that comes out of your class. Here is a list of those items which we consider to be central to the evaluation of your assessment management plan:

- Examine your groupings. Do you group flexibly to give a good variety of learning and assessment opportunities?
- Examine your assessment timing. Do you give children time on task, time to finish, time to complete (where possible) to their satisfaction as well as yours?
- Examine your sampling (see Chapter 5). For assessment purposes are you looking at too little or too much of the children's work?
- Examine your record keeping. Are all the important things, and *just* the important things going on record?
- Examine your plan in the light of school plans. Make sure you fit school strategies or you could be wasting some of your time. Any classroom organisation and management approach which undermines the continuity and progression of children through the school has to be changed. Class and whole-school plans are mutually dependent. Such plans can be refined, enhanced and developed, but only through collaborative effort.

Finally find out how well you yourself are doing. Make sure your management system delivers data which you can use to enhance your own professional development. If teachers are crudely judged on a few items of information based upon the assessment of the children, we are in a 'payment by results' situation. The best defence is to really hone your skills and make personal evaluation part of your professional function.

TEN 'MUSTS' FOR CLASS ASSESSMENT MANAGEMENT

1 The assessment of children over the year must be planned
2 Classteachers must adopt the whole-school plans
3 Teachers must keep abreast of assessment information
4 Teachers must embrace whole-school across-curriculum policies
5 Children must have access to the National Curriculum at the appropriate levels
6 Class plans for assessment must be available
7 Teachers must respect children's time on task
8 Teachers must evaluate their assessment arrangements and communicate this to the staff team
9 Assessment must enhance learning not constrain it
10 The outcome of assessment must be positive and have meaning for others, especially the children.

Summary

Our aim in writing this chapter has been to set out the major dimensions of organisation and management of assessment. There are close similarities between the concerns at the whole-school level and in the individual classroom. In both cases we see that effective planning is crucial to good practice in assessment. The outcomes of the school and class systems need to be subject to regular critical analysis.

We have not, in this chapter, attempted to go beyond highlighting the important items on the management of assessment agenda. In the next, and final chapter we go on to offer a pot-pourri of practical activities which will assist you in sorting out your own dilemmas about assessment management.

SETTING THE ASSESSMENT AGENDA: A COLLECTION OF ACTIVITIES

In this chapter we offer a number of different starting points for the creation or enhancement of your own and your school's assessment agenda. We have not organised these starting points into a particular order, neither have we set them up as a rolling programme of activities. The activities are free-standing; their only connection with each other is that they are all ways of getting inside some of the major issues to do with assessment. However, we do have thoughts about their usefulness in terms of scale and in relation to particular issues that they are most likely to highlight; suggestions about these matters accompany each activity. Most of the activities are intended for use with a staff team but some are appropriate for individual work and some could be used to support work with parents. Whoever you choose as participants, we believe that the use of any or all of these activities will enhance your insights into the major issues of assessment in your school.

In developing these activities it became clear to us that any one of the activities can act as a springboard to wider discussion of assessment issues. Your choice depends on the willingness of colleagues to participate, intellectually as well as instrumentally, and how brave you are! Try to be as creative as you can, and include strategies of the 'what if' kind which may make assumptions about the schools and situations in addition to the information you are provided with.

The activities are listed A–N. In brief, this is what they are about:

A Solving assessment dilemmas: a set of scenarios

B Disseminating information

C Amassing information using questionnaires

D Attainment targets and levels

E Topics

F Records in practice

G Listening skills

H Observation skills

I Understanding documentation

J Judgements about children's work on paper

K Creativity

L Parents

M Views about assessment from people other than teachers

N Whole-school policy

Aims   Using a set of scenarios about situations in which teachers may find themselves, the intention is for a discussion to be generated among the staff team. This discussion should highlight areas for further attention, reflection and action. Though the intent is quite serious, do not take the imaginary cases too seriously.

Participants   A group of teachers or a whole staff team.

Duration   Could be used as a one-off exercise lasting about two hours or as a springboard for a series of shorter meetings.

Procedure   Select from the set of scenarios and give a copy of the selected scenario to each member of staff a day or two before a staff meeting. They are required to read the scenario and then to write down a set of responses to the scenario. These responses should be brought to the staff meeting. Discussion of the responses can be arranged in a variety of ways; for example, each member of the staff team can proffer an observation in turn and these can be recorded. Whatever method of sharing is used, the desired outcome is that a set of differing points of view will be identified which can then be used for subsequent meetings.

A variation is to have individuals or small groups of staff look at a different scenario each and give a summary description of the scenario as well as their analysis of issues to their colleagues. The desired outcomes remain the same.

Case-study 1: Flexible timing: a whole-school approach

Vine Street Junior School is in session from 9 a.m. to 3.30 p.m. daily. It has a two class intake each year, and classes remain in year groups. There is a whole-school assembly daily starting at 9.10 a.m. which lasts 10–20 minutes. Morning break is 20 minutes long and starts at 10.30 a.m. There is one hall, used for PE, dance and as a dining hall. Resources are held centrally and small stocks are found in individual classes. There is a small school 'library' in the entrance hall, and pairs of year group classes hold year group stocks of books. The school has three computers, two on the ground floor, where there are five classrooms, and one on the first floor, where there are three classrooms and a large unused stock-room.

There is a wide variety of ways in which you can reflect on the subject of timing in Vine Street Junior. Here are some questions which may help you in compiling your list of comments and suggestions:

- How can the school timetable be set so as to make sessions as flexible as possible?
- How can the school resources be shared to assist flexible timing?
- How can the school timetable assist teacher assessment?

Case-study 2: Flexible timing within the classroom

Mrs Shanklin has a class of reception and middle infants. The fixed points in her class timetable are 10-minute breaks at 10.15 a.m. and 2.15 p.m., lunch from midday to 1.10 p.m. and a whole-school assembly at 9.45 a.m. on Fridays. There are infant and/or single class assemblies on other days, at times which she can negotiate with colleagues. Her allocation for the use of the hall is for two sessions, at 9.45 a.m. on Mondays and Tuesdays. Library, computer and TV use is negotiable. There is plenty of playground and field space which is timetable free. Here are some questions to help your reflections:

- How many notional sessions do you feel Mrs Shanklin should aspire to each day?
- Are there merits in 'clustering' her fixed points by, for example, having assembly, hall-time, TV or video and library and computer use on Mondays?
- Where are her best opportunities in the week for allowing sessions to 'overrun', and are these the best times for new learning, consolidation or assessment?
- How can Mrs Shanklin's timetabling and timing assist the assessment part of her role?

Case-study 3: Better grouping

Rose Tompkins has a class of 35 top infants. Outside the classroom door is a resource bay shared with the other two infant classes, containing books, a seating area, some imaginative play toys and the school pets. Rose can only see the bay when close to the classroom door. Her starting point for the day is in the carpeted corner opposite the door. It is to this part of the room that the children go when asked to assemble. Though the children work in groups, these have fixed membership. The children are used to a collective start and finish to each session and consult the teacher individually when they need help. The teacher works with a different group for each of four sessions in the day.

Here are some questions as starters to your thinking:

- Rose has set her groupings as whole-class and ability. What other groupings might be appropriate?
- What are the implications of work groupings for the work spaces the class has?
- Should Rose change the pattern of what children expect to do as a class, in order to modify their expectations of group work? If so, how?
- In what ways do Rose's groupings facilitate

continuous and key stage assessment?
- How could Rose best group her class for:
  teaching
  learning
  assessment?
  If there are differences between these kinds of groupings, how can they be appropriately put into use?

Case-study 4: Shared assessment management

The Junior staff at Highridge School comprise:

Miss Philpott (1st years): hard-working, conscientious, 20 years a teacher, the last ten taking this age group
Mr Price (2nd years): young, ambitious, creative ideas, but sometimes lacks application
Mrs Adamson (3rd years): very experienced, gets the girls to achieve well, has discipline problems with some boys
Mr Winner (4th years): deputy head, tries hard but needs management training, inclined to over-formality, both with the children and colleagues.

What are the strategies to try to get these people to operate a consistent overall policy and plan regarding learning opportunities and assessment? Are there, for example:

- Areas in which they may already be in accord?
- Areas in which they can work in pairs?
- Areas of the whole-school curriculum in which one of them may excel? For example, should Mrs Adamson tackle discipline and equal opportunities, or perhaps she is the last person you would ask to do this, and if so why is that?

What opportunities do you think these people need in order to arrive at a shared assessment plan? Do they need:

- Meetings in non-contact time
- Time to study and share documentation
- Regular review meetings?

What else do you think they need?

Case-study 5: Bother-free assessment

Joe Smythe is teacher of a class of fourth year juniors. He is also assessment co-ordinator for the whole school, and is anticipating being responsible for administering key stage two assessments. He is busy monitoring the development of a whole-school policy about assessment, and is looking at the installation of formal assessment in the infant department. Mrs Henessy, head of infants and teacher of the top infant class is troubled by those one or two children every year who persistently disrupt the work of others. Her concern is that teacher management of the statutory key stage assessment of other children will be severely impeded by the one or two children with behavioural difficulties. It is a problem which Mr Smythe himself may face when the children reach the end of key stage two if a solution is not found to their difficulties. What would your recommendations be to Mrs Henessy?

- Should she exclude those children from her class when she is assessing others? If so, where should those children be placed?
- Should she place a high value on assessment situation being 'normal' ones, and therefore keep disruptive children in class come what may?
- Should she rely on voluntary help to assist disruptive children while she is assessing others?

What other suggestions do you have, bearing in mind that Mrs Henessy must not limit the chances for achievement of any of the children in her care, including those with difficulties.

Activity B   A 'graffiti' board

Aims   The purpose of this activity is to generate and maintain a conversation about assessment in the everyday work of the staff.

Participants   The whole staff team, including governors and others on occasional visits.

Duration   A continuing exercise, certainly at least a school term.

Procedure   Identify a notice-board in the staffroom as being the 'anything goes on assessment' board. Talk to staff about the existence of the board and indicate that anyone is entitled to put up anything to do with assessment that they wish on the board. This could include:

- Official documents
- Newspaper cuttings
- Cartoons
- In-service courses
- Staff comments/observations
- Jokes.

In fact anything connected with assessment in the minds of individual colleagues is eligible for the assessment 'graffiti' board.

Periodically, as part of business staff meetings, the board can be 'tidied'. The process of tidying can be used as a useful source of staff discussion.

Activity C Questionnaires

Aims To solicit information about a particular aspect of assessment and to promote discussion amongst both the writers and the recipients of the questionnaire.

Participants This depends upon the information required; it could be teachers, children, parents or governors.

Duration This will vary depending on the level of control available. It is easier to set time limits within the school than with parents, for example.

Procedure Questionnaires are difficult to write. The commonest mistakes in writing them include using language which is open to widely differing interpretations, and asking more than one question within one item. For

example, to ask colleagues questions such as the following:

> 'Do you think formal assessment is a good thing?'
>
> YES/NO
>
> 'Do you think we should teach more science, and is this going to help our youngsters in their next school?'
>
> YES/NO

is asking for trouble, or at least for a headache!

So, if you are going to undertake an information collection activity using questionnaires, keep things simple and take time to reflect on the quality of your questionnaire before you rush into print.

The following extract from a short, simple questionnaire to staff on the assessment approaches they use serves to illustrate some of the work that you might undertake in a questionnaire activity.

Other questionnaires to consider include ones:

- To children about their evaluation of a topic
- To parents about what they understand about reports
- To governors about what they see to be the aims of assessment.

Please *circle* your response to the following questions:

Do you keep a diary of events in your classroom?

YES NO

If yes then
    Does the diary help with matching children to levels?
        YES! Yes yes no No NO!
    Does the diary help with reporting?
        YES! Yes yes no No NO!

Do you use tests that you produce yourself?

YES NO

Do these tests help with matching children to levels?
        YES! Yes yes no No NO!
Do the test results help with reporting?
        YES! Yes yes no No NO!

Activity D   Linking attainment targets

Aims   To look at the relationships between different attainment targets at a particular level and to analyse the implications for assessment.

Participants   Whole staff but carried out by an individual member of staff.

Duration   Difficult to determine as this is an activity that can be 'shelved' and returned to at a later date.

Procedure   Choose an AT in any of the subject areas and select a statement of attainment that seems appropriate at that time. Using the chosen statement of attainment as a first building block, search through other ATs in the same subject for building blocks that fit around the first one. Then extend your search to other subject areas. Having assembled a chart of this curriculum 'wall', present it to colleagues with a view to generating a discussion about how the children can be assessed in relation to the first building block. Figure 7.1 shows the start of such an exercise.

Figure 7.1 Linking attainment targets

	Science AT9 L3 S of A 1 S of A 3	Geography AT5 L3 S of A d L5 S of A f
Science AT2 L3 S of A 3	← Science AT9 L2 S of A 2 know that the weather has a profound effect on people's lives. →	Science AT5 L2 S of A 2

Activity E Assessing themes

Aims The purpose of this activity is to evaluate assessment approaches, procedures and possible outcomes starting with a topic or theme rather than a subject.

Participants Whole staff, but the work could contribute to a workshop with parents.

Duration The work could be arranged to coincide with the length of a chosen topic or theme. At least half a school term would be necessary and a number of staff meetings would need to include discussion of this activity on the agenda.

Procedure Choose a topic or theme and construct a topic web through a brainstorming exercise with the whole staff. This is a familiar technique in many primary schools, but for those unfamiliar with brainstorming the approach would be, in this context:

● Choose the topic through one of the following:
  past experience
  a coming event or highpoint of the year
  an interest
  provocation
  selection from an existing topic set.

It is important that all of the staff agree on the selected topic, so it is necessary to take time

over this part of the activity. Once you have done this, press on quickly into the brainstorm and keep things moving in the next phase! The process is:

● Elect a scribe
● Ensure that all staff are sure of the title of the chosen topic

The scribe writes like fury!

- Invite colleagues to throw out thoughts, feelings and ideas about the topic as quickly as possible. The scribe writes with great haste!
- When colleagues run out of things to say allow them to rest while the scribe makes a fair copy of the resultant net
- Photocopy the net, one for each member of staff
- Staff peruse the photocopy and, through discussion, refine it.

This is probably enough for one meeting. At the next meeting:

- Re-acquaint staff with the net
- Using individuals and sub-groups take parts of the net and try to establish how they link with subjects, attainment targets and statements of attainment.

Use the outcomes of the final analysis to discuss ways and means of assessing children's progress, achievement and potential in relation to the topic. The issues raised will inform teachers about topic work assessment generally. The main steps in establishing a net are shown in Figure 7.2.

Figure 7.2 Steps in establishing topic assessment

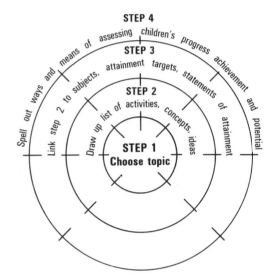

STEP 4
Spell out ways and means of assessing children's progress achievement and potential

STEP 3
Link step 2 to subjects, attainment targets, statements of attainment

STEP 2
Draw up list of activities, concepts, ideas

STEP 1
Choose topic

Activity F A record review

Aims This activity is intended to help staff appraise their own record-keeping in the context of the staff team and the development of records throughout the school.

Participants A whole school staff team.

Duration The phase of collecting and analysing information should be set up at a staff meeting. A period of time is then necessary for the assembly of initial materials. This is followed by the distribution of those materials and an opportunity for analysis. A further staff meeting is then necessary for the sharing of outcomes. Further time can then be allocated in response to the issues raised.

Procedure Using a staff meeting to launch the activity, each individual member of staff is asked to identify one child in their class who is not 'famous'. This anonymity is important and staff members should not share with other colleagues the identity of the child. Staff are then required to spend some time collecting together a report and, if appropriate, a record of achievement for that child. A photocopy of the report, with the name removed, is then made. The photocopies are distributed so that each member of the staff team has a copy of a report or set of documents about a child they do not know. The task is for each individual to prepare a picture in words, or 'pen picture' of the child from the reported information. These pen pictures are shared, in the first instance, with the member of staff who generated the data. Following the round of paired discussions a feedback session takes place involving the whole staff.

> This child is working at Level 2 in English and Level 1 in Maths. The record indicates that her speaking and listening skills are well developed. She seems well-motivated with a good orientation to her work, and the beginnings of sound study skills. The record gives little indication about how she uses her oracy and organisation skills in practical activities, for example science and art. There is some information to show that she would benefit from drama improvisations - capitalising on her oracy and relaxing her physical 'over control'.
> Current performance 'average'. Needs more creative challenge.

Activity G   Listen in

Aims   To use tape recording in order to evaluate the assessment of children's oral contributions.

Participants   Teachers and children, and then whole staff. Some of the material could support a talk to parents and governors.

Duration   This depends very much on the length of time between staff meetings but a minimum time would be about a month to obtain the data and to share it with children and colleagues.

Procedure   Depending on the number of staff, this activity should be based on pairs or groups of three teachers. For a predetermined session lasting up to about 20 minutes, each teacher should engage in a discussion with an elected group of children. It may be that the co-operation of another teacher or the head-teacher will be needed in creating the space for this discussion. The discussion should be taped. It may be, if you are not using tape recorders with the children in your class on a regular basis, that you will need a few dry runs to reduce embarrassment and 'silliness'. The tape recordings obtained should be listened to, discussed and analysed by the pair of teachers and feedback can be obtained from the children involved. Do not try to transcribe tapes for it can take at least 10 times as long as the original recording!

Activity H Observation

Aims One of the important ingredients of National Curriculum assessment is observation of children working. This activity aims to give support in developing insights into observational techniques and issues.

Participants Pairs of teachers and classes in action or the whole staff.

Duration One session and a feedback meeting, but it must be opportunistic, and take place when you have students in school or other extra pairs of hands to help you.

Procedure Ask a teacher to set up work for his or her class for a session, with the children working in groups. Two teachers from other classes can observe one of the groups, and share their observations about what went on, and how they would assess those children's performance.

A school video of children at work can be made and shown to the whole staff. All the teachers can then observe the same episodes and share their perceptions and judgements. The video also has the advantage that you can stop or replay the action, and you can all share your judgements collectively in one session.

Activity I Analysing documentation

Aims To sharpen teachers' skills in sifting through the increasing amounts of documentation that they must read.

Participants Whole staff.

Duration Teachers need time to study, so it may be planned over a week or half a term, depending on the length of the documentation and the number of staff. There should also be a feedback meeting.

Procedure Decide collectively on a range of documents or a particular document for study. Ensure there are enough copies for quick distribution. Give everyone a guide list of points. The list may, for example, include the following:

In this document:

- What are the three major points?
- What positive comments do you have?
- What criticisms do you have?
- Was it easy to understand? If not, why do you think that is?

- How did you approach it? For example, did you read the end first? What approach would have been better, now that you know what it contains?

There will be other guideline questions, depending on the documents you choose for scrutiny. If, for example, you choose the SEAC Guides to Teacher Assessment these are the kinds of pointers which may come out of a 'staff scrutiny':

- You need to decide exactly what it is that you are assessing, whether it is a specific statement of attainment or several of them
- You will need to change the way you collect assessment information according to what you are assessing
- Depending on your experience, you may need to set yourself 'practice' tasks in the short term
- Support assessment training programmes, for training can be put to good effect.

Activity J Internal moderation

Aims To open up a discussion about the extent to which there is agreement in the staff team about the levels of performance of children, based upon their work on paper.

Participants Whole staff.

Duration Two sessions with a period for collection of examples and reflection between the sessions.

Procedure In the first session use the examples of children's work provided below and on pages 110 and 111. We have given no information about age and we are not suggesting any 'grades' for the work. The examples here are prose and pictures, but in developing this activity it is important to embrace other kinds of recorded work, for example, mathem-

atics, the use of diagrams, and poetry. The supplied examples can be photocopied and used to create a set of criteria which are deemed to be important in making judgements about the levels at which the children are working. Through discussion you can identify common ground and air differences of opinion, and once this is done the staff team should commit themselves to providing a small set of examples of work from their own class for the second session. Teachers should select contributions having thought through their own opinions as to the levels of the work. Colleagues can then share their views using the set of items generated in the first session to help structure the discussion. This activity can be done in conjunction with the following one (**Assessing creativity**).

Children's work samples

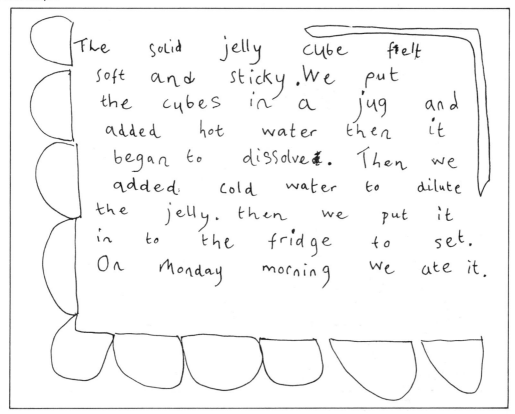

The solid jelly cube felt soft and sticky. We put the cubes in a jug and added hot water then it began to dissolve. Then we added cold water to dilute the jelly. then we put it in to the fridge to set. On Monday morning we ate it.

"Look out!" shouted the frantic helmssman. "Jive ho!". Whoosh the large wooden splintered boom lashed across the wet slippery decks. I heard one fellow sailor cry out and the short fat miserable captain yelled, "Man overboard!". There was nothing we could do about it so we just had to carry on going. Suddenly the jib which was blowing wildly broke free. I quickly scrambled over the slippery decks and dived on top of the wild jib and quickly wrapped it up with a loose haliad and put it in a sailing bag. All of a sudden the wind started to blow us of course and the mist was menacingly moving across the calm sea. Then we couldn't see where we were heading we were drifting into nowhere.

went to the gift shop. I bought a postcard for nanney, a box of maches for mummy and daddy and a little pink pig for my sister. Then we went to a place where there were lots of raptors. There was a eagle owl, a snowy owl, two falcons, an eagle, a hawk and a buzzard hawk. Next we went to petland. I saw a Shetland pony, a nanny goat, a billy goat, a lot of kids, a guine pig, two boars, fred the peacock doves and other birds, rabbits, and a calf. I was given a bag of food and I fed nearly all the animals. Some doves and pigeions ate from my hand. My friend Sarah was feeding the goats when the nanny goat bit a big hole in her bag and the greedy doves and pigions gobbled up all the food that fell out! Then we went home

Activity K Assessing creativity

Aims   To examine whether it is possible to reach a consensus about aesthetic considerations and creativity.

Participants   Whole staff.

Duration   A single session, but should be repeated periodically to remind teachers of the difficulties in assessing creativity.

Procedure   Invite every member of staff to bring along several pieces of work which may include maths, writing, models, paintings, solutions to science or technology problems, or indeed anything else they wish to bring. They should all be items which the teachers feel show creative effort. Arrange a display which everyone can look at. Discuss the implications of people's decisions, and compare the work with what might be expected at various levels of the National Curriculum. If there is consensus about the contents of the display, it can go on public display in the entrance hall!

Activity L A parents' evening

Aims   To offer the opportunity for parents to engage in some of the sort of work that their children are doing and to be supported in understanding the difficulties and the merits of making assessments which are broader than just 'marks' and 'results'. A secondary aim may be to help parents understand that assessment is difficult to do.

Participants   Staff and parents.

Duration   An evening.

Procedure   This activity makes use of an approach which a number of schools periodically adopt. Parents should be invited to take part in a practical workshop in which they have the opportunity to participate in one of three activities which are being run in parallel. The activities should be practical and involve some experimentation/problem-solving. A few examples are:

- Bridge-building
- Working with Lego®
- Junk modelling a given three-dimensional object
- Building a model using Lego-technic®
- Producing a page for the Lepidopterists' weekly newspaper.

A set time should be allocated for these activities and at the end of that time, and after a break for refreshments, parent groups should report back on their efforts and be encouraged to try to analyse the skills that they had to use. This will offer opportunities to consider the broad range of skills which are required of their children, and can be used to focus on the question 'How do we know how they are progressing?' The opportunity can be taken to show slides of children at work on similar activities.

Activity M   A role-play exercise

Aims   To explore some of the attitudes and outside perspectives that can impinge upon the school assessment principles and plans.

Participants   Staff team.

Duration   Part of an in-service day, probably a couple of hours including discussion time.

Procedure   Role-play is not to everyone's taste and gives some people a sense of threat or embarrassment. Therefore this exercise needs careful handling and, in some cases, might benefit from being run by an 'outsider'.

The situation:

A Local Education Authority has, as part of its public relations, asked heads of primary schools to hold small group meetings with a range of representatives from the local community. The purpose of these meetings is to inform representatives about developments within the work of the LEA and its schools and to obtain some feedback on how the representatives feel about these developments. The agenda (as illustrated) for this meeting within a particular school, has been arranged by the headteacher and the LEA adviser. The meeting has just reached item 3.

Present at the meeting are the headteacher (chair), LEA adviser, governor, parent governor, local business person, secondary

```
            AGENDA
1 Welcome and general intro-
  duction
2 Outline of the National
  Curriculum and how it is
  being handled by the LEA and
  this school
3 The assessment of pupils
4 Support from the local
  community
5 Feedback and closure
  followed by refreshments
```

school representative, representative from the local health centre, (and others who represent your particular environment). The numbers of each of the above will depend upon the number of staff in the school. Each member of staff draws a role from a hat and has five minutes in which to think about how the particular person they are role-playing would see item 3. No scripts are provided, nor are they necessary. After the initial 10 minutes or so of the 'meeting', when extreme points of view might be taken as staff feel their way into role, you should find that many important issues start to emerge. Besides listing these issues for subsequent use it is important to debrief the role-play participants, paying particular attention to how individual staff members felt about their 'new' perspectives.

Activity N   Writing an assessment policy document

Aims   To give help in the writing of an assessment policy document.

Participants   Individuals or groups of teachers.

Duration   Self timing.

Procedure   At a first meeting, using a brainstorming technique (see **E** on page 105 and page 64), get the staff to compile a list of all the issues to do with school assessment

policy. Ask each member of staff to note down all that they feel is relevant for their class under each of these headings. The assessment co-ordinator can collate all these contributions and compile an overall statement, which can be raised at a future meeting as an item for discussion. Once agreed, it becomes the policy guideline for all members of staff and is subject to annual review.

CONCLUSION

There is no doubt that in education these are demanding times. Never a day seems to pass when there is not an article in the newspapers or an item on the radio or television about schools and schooling. In addition, many of them seem to be critical! Whilst it is quite understandable that teachers, teacher trainers, advisers and others who are dedicated to education are bowed by the weight of criticism, it is in these times that initiatives are there to be taken. Assessment is the important ingredient that fuels much of what happens in our educational system. What right-minded teachers have to do is to grasp the assessment nettle and use it to advantage.

In order to develop assessment we have to first understand the rationale behind what is statutory and then work at bringing about change in order to satisfy ourselves that we are meeting the needs of children, as well as those of the nation! To take steps in this direction we have pin-pointed a number of the central assessment issues in this book, the most important of them being planning.

Mere chance must not be the arbiter of educational provision. Through our planning we can try to achieve some control over the future. Planning is about anticipation, forethought and action, not reaction. But in order to plan, it is necessary to look at experience as well as prescience. In assessment terms there are two essential aspects of good planning that we would like to find in more common use in our primary schools: the systematic use of experiential data, and the overt forging of connections between curriculum (as taught) and curriculum (as assessed).

Schools are awash with information. There are enough starting points for a complex set of research projects to be found in every primary school in a single morning. Teachers ignore much of this sea of data because human beings cannot cope with so much. Alas, what they choose as their focus may not be salient to all those who comment on 'standards' and 'the situation in our schools'. In order to meet allegations that we neglect the important things in assessment, we need to become much more rigorous about collecting the data around us. We also have to take seriously the things we find, even if they do not conform to our own or others' prejudices and expectations. The construction of school data bases seems to us to be an essential part of this active planning process.

In addition to the formation of data bases, teachers must analyse and really reflect on the *process* of school, in addition to its *product*. The history of assessment, which has its roots in specific views about human nature, mitigates against a consideration of educational process. An over-emphasis on product and objectives prevents the development of a whole range of human talents in our children. The National Curriculum is on the brink of becoming an objectives based approach – it is only the enlightened teacher in the forward-looking school who defends breadth of experience, sensitivity and creativity for all of our children. We must all do our utmost to avoid the stereotyping and inappropriate characterisation of children under the assessment template.

114

So what of the future? Cynicism has no place in education, since its rationale is embedded in the future. We have to look forward, and do so with energy and positive expectations. Starting with what might appear to be very small but nonetheless important steps, we would suggest that teachers and schools might view the future as being concerned with:

- An appreciation that children's work should be sampled and not treated exhaustively
- An extension of kinds of assessment well beyond what children can write down
- The use of broad profiles of achievement rather than narrow subject-based 'examination' results.

We should reach a point in the not too distant future, when we can look back on the 1990s as marking the beginning of the time when there grew ways of assessing that took account of children as whole developing people, and not just 'candidates' to imbue with knowledge and experience. This book cannot make that happen, but we hope that it will help.

Bibliography

CLEMSON, D. and CLEMSON, W., *The Really Practical Guide to National Curriculum 5–11* (Stanley Thornes, 1989)

CLIFT, P. *et al., Record Keeping in Primary Schools* (Macmillan, 1981)

DEAN, J., *Organising Learning in the Primary School Classroom* (Croom Helm, 1983)

DES and the Welsh Office (HMSO):
Education Reform Bill [Bill 53] (1987)

Circular No 17/89: The Education (School Records) Regulations (1989)

Circular No 8/90: Records of Achievement (1990)

The Education (Individual Pupils' Achievement) (Information) Regulations (1990)

Draft: The Education Reform Act 1988: National Curriculum: Order under Section 4 for Assessment Arrangements in English, Mathematics and Science at Key Stage 1 (May 1990)

SEAC, *A Guide To Teacher Assessment Packs A, B and C* (Heinemann Educational for SEAC 1990)

Keyword index